THE ORGANIC AND
THE INNER WORLD

The Organic and the Inner World is one of a series of books under the title PSYCHOANALYTIC **ideas** which brings together the best of Public Lectures and other writings given by analysts of the British Psycho-Analytical Society on important psychoanalytic subjects.

Other titles in the Psychoanalytic ideas Series:

"You Ought To!"—A Psychoanalytic Study of the Superego and Conscience
Bernard Barnett

Autism in Childhood and Autistic Features in Adults:
A Psychoanalytic Perspective
Kate Barrows (editor)

Child Analysis Today
Luis Rodriguez De la Sierra (editor)

Shame and Jealousy: The Hidden Turmoils
Phil Mollon

Time and Memory
Rosine J. Perelberg

Spilt Milk: Perinatal Loss and Breakdown
Joan Raphael-Leff (editor)

Symbolization: Representation and Communication
James Rose (editor)

Unconscious Phantasy
Riccardo Steiner (editor)

Psychosis (Madness)
Paul Williams (editor)

Psychoanalytic Ideas and Shakespeare
Inge Wise and Maggie Mills (editors)

Adolescence
Inge Wise (editor)

THE ORGANIC AND THE INNER WORLD

edited by
Ronald Doctor and Richard Lucas

KARNAC

First published in 2009 by
Karnac Books Ltd
118 Finchley Road, London NW3 5HT

British Library Cataloguing in Publication Data

A C.I.P. for this book is available from the British Library

ISBN: 978 1 85575 651 9

Edited, designed and produced by The Studio Publishing Services Ltd,
www.publishingservicesuk.co.uk
e-mail: studio@publishingservicesuk.co.uk

Printed in Great Britain

www.karnacbooks.com

CONTENTS

In memory of our friend and colleague Richard Lucas

SERIES EDITORS' FOREWORD

The Psychoanalytic Ideas series of books, now well established and widely read among practitioners, has always tried to bring together original thinkers for the purpose of exploring cutting edge conceptualization in psychoanalysis. The origin of the series goes back a long way to an early predecessor, the "Winter Lectures" held at the British Psychoanalytical Society, in which public lectures given by certain members of the Society were gathered together and published in pamphlet form. These lectures were often "work in progress", in which the analysts developed new ideas or communicated their understanding of the latest developments in psychoanalysis. Today, the Psychoanalytic Ideas series takes this tradition forward by encouraging analysts who are working on interesting and important themes and ideas to bring them to fruition via the series.

This latest Psychoanalytic Ideas volume, ably edited by Ronald Doctor and the late Richard Lucas, succeeds in generating fascinating debates around some of the most intractable and profound conditions that can afflict the psyche and soma. Relations between the body and the mind, the object-relations and attachment crises in borderline personality disorder, the origins of bi-polar disorder (manic–depressive psychosis) and its devastating effects on think-ing, and the complex psychological and physical problems of dementia are addressed in unusual depth by some of the foremost writers in psychoanalysis. The outcome of these debates is a sense of hope that these difficult subjects can yield levels of understand-ing and meaning that both advance psychoanalysis and, more importantly, lead to improved ways of treating those who suffer.

Inge Wise and Paul Williams
Series Editors

Robin Anderson, MRCP, FRCPsych, is a training analyst in adult, and child and adolescent analysis at the Institute of Psychoanalysis, where he has also been head of the child and adolescent psychoanalytic training. He was Consultant Child and Adolescent Psychiatrist at the Tavistock Clinic from 1991 until 2000 and was head of the Adolescent Department. He now concentrates on teaching and working in private psychoanalytic practice. He has edited two books: *Clinical Lectures on Klein and Bion*, and *Facing It Out: Clinical Perspectives on Adolescent Disturbance*, with Anna Dartington (Routledge, to be published in May 2009). He has a particular interest in early object relationships and he has applied this in working with suicidal and self-harming young people.

Anthony W. Bateman, MA, FRCPysch, is Consultant Psychiatrist in Psychotherapy (Haringey), Halliwick Unit, Barnet, Enfield, and Haringey Mental Health Trust, Visiting Professor, University College, London, and Visiting Consultant, Menninger Clinic, Baylor College of Medicine, Houston, USA. His research interest is in personality disorder and he has published many research papers on the topic. His books include *Introduction to Psychotherapy: An Outline* *of Psychodynamic Principles and Practice* (2001), with Dennis Brown and Jonathan Pedder, *Psychotherapy of Borderline Personality Disorder: Mentalization Based Treatment* (2004) and *Mentalization Based Therapy for Borderline Personality Disorder: A Practical Guide* (2006), both with Peter Fonagy, and *Mentalization in Clinical Practice* (2008), with Jon Allen and Peter Fonagy.

Ronald Britton is well known internationally as a psychoanalytic writer, teacher, and clinician. His books include *The Oedipus Complex Today; Belief and Imagination; Sex, Death and the Superego.* He was President of the British Psychoanalytical Society, a Vice-President of the International Psychoanalytical Association and former Chair of the Deptartment for Children and Families, Tavistock Clinic.

Ronald Doctor, FRCPsych, is Consultant Psychiatrist in Psycho-therapy at the West London Mental Health NHS Trust, Chair of the NHS Liaison Committee, British Psychoanalytical Society, Chair of the Association of the Psychoanalytical Psychotherapists in the NHS (APP), Academic Secretary of the Psychotherapy Faculty, Royal College of Psychiatrists and Honorary Clinical Lecturer, Imperial College London. He has a particular interest in forensic psychotherapy, and he has edited two books: *Dangerous Patients: A Psychodynamic Approach to Risk Assessment and Management* (2003); and *Murder: A Psychotherapeutic Investigation* (2008).

Sandra Evans is Consultant in Old Age Psychiatry at East London Foundation NHS Trust, and Senior Lecturer in Psychiatry at Barts and the London School of Medicine & Dentistry at Queen Mary, University of London. She qualified as a Group Analyst in 1998, and is a member of the Group Analytic Network. She is current head of the older adult section of the APP. She has co-edited a book on dynamic psychotherapy with older people, *Talking Over the Years* (2004).

Peter Fonagy, PhD, FBA, is Freud Memorial Professor of Psycho-analysis and Head of the Research Department of Clinical, Educa-tional and Health Psychology at University College London; Chief Executive of the Anna Freud Centre, London; and Consultant to the Child and Family Program at the Menninger Department of

Psychiatry and Behavioral Sciences at the Baylor College of Medicine, Houston, USA. He is Chair of the Postgraduate Education Committee of the International Psychoanalytic Association and a Fellow of the British Academy. He is a clinical psychologist and a training and supervising analyst in the British Psychoanalytical Society in child and adult analysis. His work integrates empirical research with psychoanalytic theory, and his clinical interests centre around borderline psychopathology, violence, and early attachment relationships. He has published over 300 chapters and articles and has authored or edited several books. His most recent books include *What Works for Whom? A Critical Review of Psychotherapy Research* (with A. Roth); *Mentalization-Based Treatment for Borderline Personality Disorder: A Practical Guide* (with Anthony Bateman); *Handbook of Mentalization-Based Treatment* (with Jon Allen); *Mentalizing in Clinical Practice* (with Jon Allen and Anthony Bateman); and *Social Cognition and Developmental Psychopathology* (with Carla Sharp and Ian Goodyer).

Roger Kennedy is Consultant Psychiatrist at the Cassel Hospital Family Service, Honorary Senior Lecturer in Psychiatry, Imperial College London, Training Analyst, British Psychoanalytical Society, Past President, British Psychoanalytical Society, author of many papers and eleven books, the latter including *Psychotherapists as Expert Witnesses* (2005), *The Many Voices of Psychoanalysis* (2007) and *Couch Tales* (2008).

Leon Kleimberg is a training analyst for the British Psychoanalytical Society. He is a Visiting Lecturer at the Tavistock Clinic Adult Department and a Visiting Lecturer on the MSc course in Psychoanalytic Studies at University College London. He has published papers in the UK and abroad in areas of psychoanalysis and creativity, psychoanalysis and psychopathology, and psychoanalysis and immigration.

Richard Lucas was Consultant Psychiatrist at St Anne's Hospital and a member of the British Psychoanalytical Society. He had a particular interest in the integration of analytic concepts within general psychiatry and has written on many related subjects, including the psychotic wavelength, puerperal psychosis, and cyclical psychosis.

He received the OBE in 2003 for his contribution to the Disability Living Allowance Award Board.

Trudie Rossouw is a psychoanalyst and a Consultant Child and Adolescent Psychiatrist, working in North East London Foundation Trust where she is also the Associate Medical Director for Specialist Services.

Margot Waddell is a member of the British Psychoanalytical Society and a Consultant Child and Adolescent Psychotherapist in the Adolescent Department, Tavistock Clinic, London. She teaches and lectures both in Britain and abroad, she has written widely in the field of psychoanalysis and child psychotherapy and edits the Tavistock Clinic Book Series. A new and extended edition of her book *Inside Lives: Psychoanalysis and the Growth of the Personality* was published by Karnac in 2002, and more recently, in 2005, *Understanding 12–14 Year Olds*, published by Jessica Kingsley.

PREFACE

Roger Kennedy

For some years, there has been an unfortunate tendency in the UK for psychiatry and psychoanalysis to be perceived as in opposition to one another, to the detriment of both disciplines. Rather than see "organic" psychiatry on one side and "dynamic" psychiatry on the other, the British Psychoanalytical Society now wishes to try to foster closer links between psychoanalysis and psychiatry. To this end, psychoanalysts have been going out to give presentations of their work to various psychiatric departments, in the hope of building up increasing understanding of both current developments in analytic thinking, and how analysts can learn from psychiatric colleagues. Topics presented have included analytic work with psychotic patients, comparisons between analytic work and CBT, risk assessments of children from an analytic perspective, and detailed clinical presentations of work with disturbed patients.

2007 was the 150th anniversary of Freud's birth, and this presented an opportunity to show how relevant much of Freud's thought is today, despite the view often expressed by some psychiatrists at least, not to mention parts of the media, that Freud is "old hat". In fact, our experience of putting on a number of Freud events was that there is a great hunger to know more about psychoanalysis, particularly among young people, both those in psychiatric training and in the wider community. In parts of the academic world, there is a particular interest in psychoanalysis; indeed, the most subscribed courses in some of our most prestigious universities are those where psychoanalysis is involved. The British Psychoanalytical Society is currently actively engaged in fostering exchanges with a number of distinguished academics with a particular interest in psychoanalysis.

As part of the Freud celebrations, our National Health Service (NHS) liaison committee, chaired by Dr Richard Lucas, organized what turned out to be a popular and fascinating conference on the 13th May 2007, "The Organic and Inner World", which aimed to tackle the unhelpful division between psychiatry and psychoanalysis. Dr Ronald Doctor was responsible for much of the organization of the day, where a number of excellent papers were presented that revealed the subtle way that psychoanalysis is able to examine the complex nature of the mind and its disturbances. Not only were different conditions examined, such as borderline personality disturbance, dementia, and manic-depression, but different approaches to tackling the mind and the mind–body boundary were also displayed, revealing the rich variety of current analytic thinking.

The day began with a masterly overview of the field of mind and matter by Dr Ronald Britton. He locates psychoanalysis and psychiatry on a conceptual axis formed by putting the realms of the physical and the mental at opposite ends of a continuum, which, as yet, does not meet in the middle. At present, the neurosciences are approaching from one end and psychoanalysts from the other end. Freud began by trying to create a psychology for neurologists, in his "Project for a scientific psychology", but then abandoned this for a new focus on subjective experience. Britton makes the important point that, though analysts occupy the subjective position, we should be facing towards the other end, not turning our backs on it. Indeed, as he points out, the temptation at either end of the axis is for each to turn their back on the other. As our patients live in the middle, this would seem to be most unfortunate.

For Britton, psychoanalysis is a discipline that straddles the "untidy" middle ground, where we actually live. Yet, we should not be blind to what is going on at either end of the continuum, particularly when there arise opportunities to make connecting links between different ends.

The middle ground, for Britton, concerns most particularly the area of belief. Psychoanalysis deals with those "lurking beliefs of the night . . . those ghosts that vanish when we subject ourselves to the sharply focused light of educated reason".

In contrast to the attempt to overcome beliefs, such as in cognitive–behavioural therapy (CBT), the aim of analysis is to find the hidden beliefs of our patients and to help them relinquish them.

The work of Professor Peter Fonagy and Dr Anthony Bateman on mentalization highlights a particular development of psychoanalytic thought that has grown out of attachment theory, itself a product of John Bowlby's psychoanalytically informed empirical research on maternal deprivation. Much of their own research, which is influenced by psychological and neurological findings, is based upon work with borderline personality disordered (BPD) patients. BPD is a complex and serious mental disorder, characterized by "a pervasive pattern of difficulties with emotion regulation, impulse control, and instability both in relationships and in self-image, with a mortality rate associated with suicide that is fifty times that of the general population". Fonagy and Bateman make the point that the regulation of "emotion and the catastrophic reaction to the loss of intensely invested social ties together place borderline personality disorder in the domain of attachment".

Their closely argued paper gives substantial evidence for seeing BPD as arising from a deficit in attachment-related mentalization; that is, that such patients have a limited capacity to comprehend and use their knowledge of their own and others' states of mind. They also suggest a model of how such deficits are caused, when, for example, in constitutionally vulnerable individuals, there is a problem in mirroring the baby's experiences.

They suggest that psychotherapy "has the potential to recreate an interactional matrix of attachments in which mentalization develops and flourishes. The therapist's mentalizing in a way that fosters the patient's mentalizing is seen as a critical facet of the therapeutic relationship and the essence of the mechanism of change. The crux of the value of psychotherapy is the experience of another human being's having the patient's mind in mind. This, of course, brings one back to Freud's simple yet radical idea, that listening to patients in the context of a relationship was therapeutic.

Dr Sandra Evans' moving paper on the unconscious in dementia provides evidence for the omnipresent nature of unconscious processes in the brain-damaged, demented patient. She shows with illuminating examples how speculating on the mental life of a person who is losing their mind assists our understanding of the patient's experience. This can be helpful not only in understanding the patient, but also in enabling the patient's carers to have more understanding of the patient's difficulties and vulnerabilities, which can enable the patients themselves to receive better care.

This is a difficult area for all to face, and where we can see the clear interaction between brain pathology and its psychological effects. As Evans points out, anxiety about our own future old age causes us to ignore the communications of those who are slowed or altered by disease, but present, none the less. She points out that working with "dementia sufferers using an analytic framework, which is based on an acceptance of unconscious processes, enriches the task. It improves the quality of life for all concerned, and might provide another window through which to understand the mind, in all of is many states".

Dr Trudie Rossouw provides us with a fascinating and detailed account of the taxing psychoanalysis of a manic-depressive patient. It is "an exploration of the psychic life of an illness in which psychiatric research strongly suggests the existence of organic pathology". Yet, this does not exclude the use of psychoanalytic understanding, which can be complementary. As she puts it eloquently:

> Psychoanalysis offers something unique for it allows us to observe and come closer to understanding the intimate subjective experience . . . of our patients' minds. A patient suffering from manic-depressive illness lives a stormy life. Their internal and external relationships are influenced as the affective tides inherent in the cyclical phases of the condition change. However, this is also our opportunity; our challenge is to see if analytic treatment can alter the intensity of the storms and render them less dangerous.

Through her sensitive and firm handling of the transference and countertransference with this ill patient, Rossouw presents the complex interaction between the illness and the personality of the patient, helping the patient to become less suicidal. Her complex yet clear paper provided a fitting end to a fascinating day and to this collection of papers, which, one hopes, will provide guidance and inspiration to other practitioners in the mental health field.

Introduction

Richard Lucas and Ronald Doctor

On the 13th May 2006, a conference was held at the Institute of Psychoanalysis, entitled "The Organic and the Inner World". It was organized by the National Health Service (NHS) Liaison Committee of the British Psychoanalytical Society. Its aim was to consider the place for analytic thinking in the world of psychiatry, with its emphasis on an organic approach to major psychiatric disorders.

In a psychiatric world dominated by evidence based medicine, there is a realization by many that the inner world is a far more complex proposition than can be related to solely through a reductionistic approach. At the same time, as verified throughout the papers, the organic and the analytic approach are not placed in opposition, but both have their own unique contributions. In the book, we have kept the format as for the original conference: that is, that there are four seminal papers, followed by responses from the opening discussants, which amount to original contributions in their own right.

In his chapter "Mind and matter: a psychoanalytic perspective", Ron Britton brilliantly sets the scene through helping us to think about this whole area. He points out the body–mind problem is one of philosophy's unresolved issues; neuroscientists are approaching from one end and psychoanalysts from the other. He reminds us how Freud started as a neuroscientist before moving over to study the inner world. He points out the danger of half-truths; while our views might be correct, the opposing view should also be considered. He thinks that this has been the case with dynamic and organic psychiatry where "both sides were in the right with what they affirmed, though wrong in what they denied". This is why we should turn our faces towards the organic, not away from it, while exploring the mind.

In a considered response to Britton's paper, Leon Kleimberg acknowledges Britton's description of the importance of belief and uncertainty as a forerunner to knowledge. He also emphasizes that, "as Freud suggested, an important aspect in the process that gives birth to the mind and keeps its links with the body and the object is the affective or emotional response". In a delightful vignette, Kleimberg highlights the absurdity of attempting to set up mind as more important than matter. He had asked a sixteen-year-old adolescent boy, as part of a research project, which was of more importance to him, his mind or his body. The boy's response was, "What kind of question is that. I don't know . . . it is like asking who is more important, my mother or father . . . they are actually both equally important in their own way . . . Mum does the looking after . . . dad helps with the discipline!"

At the conference Peter Fonagy gave a lively and masterful presentation, linking attachment theory to activated areas of the brain. He demonstrated how certain areas of the brain light up with well-grounded, maternally based, attachment behaviour. In contrast, in romantic love all the well-grounded areas turn off and another part of the brain lights up, showing indeed that love is blind rather than well thought through!

For this book, we are fortunate to have available, through the courtesy of the *Journal of Clinical Psychology*, the recent paper published jointly by Fonagy with Anthony Bateman that reviews the mechanisms of change in mentalization-based treatment of borderline personality disorder and links it with demonstrable changes in activity within the brain.

Robin Anderson's response was to describe how he was influenced by Henri Rey at the Maudsley in finding for himself that the analytic pathway, rather than the organic one, became his way forward. In analytic work, change comes from the ability to bear psychic pain and frustration, and sometimes Anderson argues that the neurobiological approach, in their findings, may at times appear too simplistic, but that there is a debate to be had and that a creative dialogue is vital for both sides of this mind–body barrier.

Trudie Rossouw provides a rare opportunity to share an analytic experience with a patient suffering from a manic-depressive illness living a stormy life. While psychiatric research strongly suggests the existence of organic pathology, she argues that psychoanalysis offers something unique in observing the intimate subjective experience (conscious and unconscious) of our patients' minds. In detailed sessional material, she illustrates how she was able to point out to the patient that she was playing a dangerous game of Russian roulette with her mind and the therapy when contemplating taking an overdose.

In his commentary on Rossouw's paper, Richard Lucas underlines how relating to such difficult, intransigent states of mind can be a soul-destroying experience for analysts, accounting for why so few such cases are to be found in the analytic literature. Yet, it is no bad thing that one's delusions of omnipotence and cherished beliefs are shattered and we have to think again about what is happening. He argues that analytic insights have a lot to offer in general psychiatry, provided we attune in a realistic way.

Sandra Evans gives a sensitive presentation on dementia, and how using an analytic framework, which is based on an acceptance of unconscious processes, enriches the task, and might provide another window through which to understand the working of the mind in all of its many states. Among other clinical examples, she illustrates how the patient's past experiences and inner worlds affect their presentation when struggling with the effects of Alzheimer's. She contrasted two patients' reactions to mirrors in their homes. One looked in the mirror and said that she had a helpful neighbour caring for her, though there was none in reality. Another, with a less secure internal world, experienced persecutory figures in the mirror.

In a thoughtful response to Evan's paper, Margot Waddell points out how, in dementia, as the protections of habit and assumptive ability and capacity fall away, often an unresolved oedipal situation emerges with expressions of jealousy and fear of abandonment. She provides an illustrative vignette. Fears are projected into the carers and the importance of maintaining a sensitive empathy is emphasized by both Evans and Waddell.

CHAPTER ONE

Mind and matter: a psychoanalytic perspective

Ronald Britton

T he title suggests this might be a treatise on philosophy's oldest debates: realism *vs.* idealism or physicality *vs.* ideality; and it raises one of philosophy's unresolved issues: the body–mind problem. I am not a philosopher and I will not be pursuing the argument between materialism and idealism, but trying to locate psychoanalysis and psychiatry on a conceptual axis formed by putting physical and mental at opposite ends of a continuum which as yet does not meet in the middle. The approach to the join has to be from one or the other end. At the present time, the neurosciences are approaching from one end and we in psychoanalysis from the other: somewhere between 1895 and 1900 Freud changed ends. In 1895 he wrote that he was totally involved in his "Psychology for neurologists", a project for a scientific psychology (Freud, 1895). It was a brilliant speculative attempt that was never finalized or published. By 1900 and his publication of the *Interpretation of Dreams* (1900a), he was, and would remain, at the other end of my imputed axis. At his new starting point it was not neurones but ideas that were the atoms of his inquiry, and information about them came from dreams, the psychopathology of everyday life, self-analysis, literature, mythology, and clinical experience with neurotic patients. Another version of this axis has subjectivity at one end and objectivity at the other.

Ever since Freud changed ends we have occupied the subjective position. However, we should be facing towards the other end, *not* turning our backs on it. The temptation at either end of this axis is to turn one's back on the other. This has been so at times in psychiatry, where so-called organic psychiatry is at one end and dynamic psychiatry at the other, and the temptation is for each to turn its back on the other. As our patients live in the middle, this would seem to me to be unfortunate.

I am speaking as a practising analyst, not a philosopher, but, as William Massicote, who is a philosopher, says in a paper entitled "The surprising philosophical complexity of psychoanalysis (belatedly acknowledged)", "Psychoanalysis encounters virtually every philosophical problem" (Massicote, 1995). Psychoanalysis has, like other professional disciplines, established its own way of proceeding and a discourse proper to itself inside which it can conduct its inquiries and arguments in its own terms. You could say the same about quantum mechanics: once under way it has pursued its own mathematical equations in its own way without having to reconcile its quantum logic with anything outside its realm of sub-atomic particle physics. However, just as quantum mechanics has to meet up with large body physics and cosmology at some point, so we in psychoanalysis have to meet up with psychiatry. When we do meet, I think we need to be clear about the unarticulated philosophical position we adopt as we approach questions about the relationship of brain to mind, or between psychoanalysis and organic psychiatry.

Everyone approaches these fundamental questions from some personal direction, so let me state my professional background and my theoretical position at the outset. My principal interests from school onwards have been in biology and literature. I started out in general medicine and I was fortunate in gaining some specialist knowledge of neurology working as a junior doctor at Queen's Square before I trained in adult and child psychiatry. From psychiatry, I moved eventually to full time psychoanalytic practice. My past experience, therefore, includes physical and mental disorders, but for the past thirty years it has been psychoanalytic.

My own theoretical position on the body–mind question is that I believe in psychogenesis: that is, that ideas can produce effects. I also believe in somato-psychic phenomena: that is, that bodily processes can give rise to mental states. This probably sounds obvious, but actually not everyone believes both of these propositions.

Epiphenomenalism, a term invented by Darwin's most enthusiastic follower, T. H. Huxley, asserts that mental phenomena are *only* the accompanying experience of physical events; that ideas, beliefs, etc., do not cause *anything* in themselves. I think some psychiatric schools base themselves on that thoroughgoing physicalism, and regard mental states as simply experiential accompaniments to physical events, rather like the bang of thunder and the flash of lightning are the perceptual accompaniments of electrical discharge. We also find others who intellectually inhabit the other end of the body–mind axis and see the physical world as just a mental construction. Thoroughgoing philosophical "idealism" holds that reality is in its nature mental or spiritual. Blake, for example, claimed, "Mental things alone are real". "Science", he said, "is the tree of death". The eye is an organ for projection not perception:

> This Life's dim Windows of the Soul
> Distorts the Heavens from Pole to Pole
> And leads you to believe a Lie
> When you see with, not thro' the Eye
> [Keynes, 1959, p. 753]

Although this is no longer fashionable in full fig, as it was in some nineteenth century metaphysics, it underlies some modern styles of thought such as existentialism and hermeneutics, various postmodern, holistic, neo-platonic ideas, and the wilder shores of alternative medicine. Psychoanalysis finds itself straddling physicalism and mentalism, or, as I prefer to put it, occupying the middle ground between them. This ground has been vacated by natural science at one end and by analytical philosophy at the other. Both of them, in search of rigour and precision, have excluded anything outside their own confined area of inquiry, thus leaving unoccupied the intellectual territory in between. They have made great strides by doing this, and produced intellectually impressive results. However, one could say that, although it is conceptually unsatisfactory, this untidy middle ground is where we actually live. When we are not at work in the laboratory, in our seminars, or at our desks, we lead personal lives. Whatever deterministic physicalist formulation or reality-dissolving idealism we espouse at work, once we are at home we attribute to ourselves and to others psychological motives and we react to what we believe to be facts; and, even in those demarcated areas of intellectual inquiry, the laboratory or the lecture room, the personal all too often intrudes, bringing with it a rich mixture of body and mind.

It was pointed out by John Stuart Mill that the split between realism and idealism is as old as philosophy itself. He wrote of an eternal dispute between those who look to innate ideas as the source of knowledge and those who assert that

> sensation and experience are the sole materials of our knowledge . . . Sensualism is the common term of abuse for the one philosophy, mysticism for the other. The one doctrine is accused of making men beasts, the other lunatics. [Leavis, 1950, p. 111]

Plato represents the same conflict as the

> Battle of the gods and the giants—one side drags everything down from heaven and the unseen to earth . . . those who battle against them [contend] that true existence consists in certain incorporeal forms which are the objects of the mind. [Flew, 1979, p. 36]

For Plato the "Forms", that is, innate ideas, preceded experience. They were "changeless eternal non-sensible objects" that inform our sensuous experience, which gives us only a dim view of them. He expressed it in the myth of the cave as a metaphorical description of human enlightenment.

> The prisoners in the Cave are at first chained to face the back wall where all they can see are shadows, cast by a fire which is behind them, of themselves and of objects which are carried between them and the fire. Later they manage to turn round and they see the fire and the objects which cast the shadows. Later still they escape from the Cave, see the outside world in the light of the sun, and finally the sun itself. The sun represents the Forms of the Good in whose light the truth is seen; it reveals the world, hitherto invisible, and is also the source of life. [Murdoch, 1977, p. 4]

I am sure you can recognize countless offspring from Plato's ideal-istic philosophy even within our own sphere; one could say that Jung was much more Platonic than Freud, and currently there is an argument amongst devotees of Bion between those who prefer his early writings and those who espouse his later work, where he is a more thoroughgoing Platonist.

The separation of physical and mental, or, as it might have been put then, material and spiritual, crystallized in the seventeenth cen-tury in Descartes's dualism. "Cogito ergo sum", familiar to all as, "I think therefore I am", and "sum res cogitans", "I am a being whose nature is to think and whose being requires no place and depends on no material thing". These two independent worlds, one of spirit and the other body, were, Descartes thought, possibly connected through that unlikely organ, the pineal gland. Cartesian thinking is regarded as misguided in this country and, in the 1940s, Gilbert Ryle did a much acclaimed demolition job on Descartes with his description of the "ghost in the machine" and his linguistic analy-sis that affirmed that Descartes made a "category mistake" by regarding mind as a different member of the same class of things as body (Ryle, 1949). Mental life, Ryle asserts, has no counterpart to physical space, so to use the language of space is a category mis-take. Also, for Ryle, mental activity is not antecedent to the effects it brings about, but is the sum of its manifestations. Mind, in other words, is what it does. It does not cause things to happen. Cause and effect, derived from the study of physical machines, he said, is another category mistake. I think he threw the baby out with the bathwater, but his ideas had a big influence on the reductionist tendency of British psychiatry and provided an intellectual back-ground to cognitive–behavioural therapy. I can see why that title has wide appeal in our psycho-phobic, objectively obsessed coun-try, but, to my subjectivist mind, "cognitive–behavioural" sounds like an oxymoron.

Personally, I follow Bion in regarding thoughts as anterior to thinking; thinking, he asserts, has developed to deal with thoughts. These thoughts are generated from sense impressions, biologically derived phantasies, pre-conceptions, and memories.

Ryle distinguished between knowledge and belief. However, when doing so, he limited knowledge to "knowing how" and dis-missed "knowing that" to the realm of "belief". "Roughly", he says, "believe [sic] is of the same family as motive words, where 'know' is of the same family as skill words." "So we ask", he says, "how a person knows this, but only why a person believes that, as we ask how a person ties a clove hitch, but why he wants to tie a clove-hitch". I will return to the subject of belief later, as I take the view, like Ryle, that all we have is belief in this world, but I would add that our sense of security depends on our innate capacity to treat it as knowledge. However, to return to Ryle, his attitude of subtle contempt for anything subjective, which he shares with some parts of British psychiatry, is best conveyed with a quotation:

> Overt intelligent performances are not clues to the workings of minds; they are those workings. Boswell described Johnson's mind when he described how he wrote, talked, ate, fidgeted and fumed. His description was, of course, incomplete, since there were notoriously some thoughts which Johnson kept carefully to himself and there must have been many dreams, daydreams, and silent babblings which only Johnson could have recorded *and only a James Joyce would have wished him to have recorded.* [Ryle, 1949, p. 57, my italics]

As well as disposing of the relevance of the subjective, that certainly puts Joyce in his place, and, of course, Freud, though Ryle pays homage to Freud elsewhere. He hails him as "psychology's one man of genius", only to use that to assert that he belongs in a "medical category" and that psychology as a counterpart to physiology does not really exist (*ibid.*, p. 305).

It is easy to demolish dualism, perhaps, but not so easy to replace it. Spinoza, the seventeenth century father of pantheism, with God as Nature, took it that there is only one infinite substance and that mind and matter are different attributes: like one man known by two names, not two separate men. Leibniz's view was that there are an infinite number of substances, monads, all separately maintained by God, to whom they are related, without any interaction between them; an odd image, rather like a large family of only children.

If we discard dualism *and* theism, we are left with various forms of parallelism in which mental and physical coexist in a non-causal relationship, or some sort of Monism, that is, the belief that only one kind of substance exists. This allows materialists to assert that all is material and idealists that all is mental. "Neutral monism", espoused by William James, is probably the concept with which we are most comfortable; it suggests that there is one common substance of which matter and mind are phenomenal modifications.

A more modern version might be to take pattern or sequence as non-material features of physical substance. The effect of a code is, after all, independent of the nature of the material carrying the code, but it does need some substance and it does travel through physical space. In a way, this could be said to be true of DNA: it is a code based on sequence, and one that can be reproduced through various chemical transformations. However clever our abstractions, what Braithwaite calls our scientific deductive systems, we are never at ease without an analogical model. Braithwaite warns us of the risks of misconceptions that come from using models, such as mistaking the inherent properties of the model for the logic of the system it is meant to represent and concluding, thereby, that something is self evident which really pertains to the model, not the scientific deductive system (Braithwaite, 1946). Nevertheless, we find comfort and conviction using them, and our familiarity with computers offers us a new model for the old problem. We can now distinguish between hard- and software, a distinction that has already crept into that most reliable lexicon, jargon, where we now speak of faults in the "hard wiring" to distinguish brain deficits from psychic dysfunction.

However much it was scoffed at as a philosophical position, dualism was nevertheless institutionalized by the separation of physical science from the philosophy of mind and the separation of physics from metaphysics in the nineteenth century. Once liberated from each other, they were free to progress within the perimeter of the field they defined for themselves. In effect, I think the professionals have solved their problem by confining their activities to their own zone of rigour and expertise. This tends to result in the big questions being left to amateurs. A hundred years before Freud began to build psychoanalysis, its precursors, the poets and thinkers of the Romantic Movement, tried to deal with the big questions that had been left on one side by the rationality of the eighteenth century "Enlightenment". Of these, the most outstandingly original thinker was the poet Coleridge. Born in 1752, he formed an intellectual partnership with Wordsworth in 1797 that resulted in the lyrical Ballads, exactly a hundred years before Freud first described the Oedipus complex in a letter to Fleiss. Not only did Coleridge write haunting, memorable poetry, such as "The Ancient Mariner", "Kubla Khan", and "Christobel", but he brought German philosophy to England, particularly that of Kant, to rebut the narrowness of English Utilitarianism. Thanks to some marvellous scholarship by Kathleen Coburn, we now have access to his previously uncollected and unpublished "notebooks", where he privately jotted down his ideas about everything (Coburn, 1961). He was proto-psychoanalytic: not only did he think of unconscious ideas and motives, attached importance to dreams and to the formative importance of childhood experience, he surprises one with his invention of words such as psychosomatic and pre-conception. For our present purposes, I will quote three short passages.

> A passion is a state of emotion having its immediate cause not in Things but in our thoughts of the Things—A passion is a state of emotion which whatever its object or occasion may be, in ourselves or out of ourselves, has its proper and immediate cause not in this but in our Thoughts respecting it . . . [Coburn, 1951, p. 66]

For Coleridge, thought is the intermediary of experience and self-awareness is the key to understanding. And yet he wrote:

> The mischievous yet logical consequences of the Cartesian Dogma [is] the separation of Psychology from physiology, depriving the former of all root and objective truth, and reducing the latter to a mere enumeration of facts and phenomena without copula or living form. [ibid., p. 65]

He also has thoughts which are precursors of the ideas on symbolism and symbolic equation of Hanna Segal, and of Winnicott's transitional object. He wrote:

> Art might itself be defined as of a middle quality between a thought and a thing . . . In every work of art there is a reconcilement of the external with the internal. [ibid., p. 209]

The Romantic Movement's agenda, to include in secular discourse what had previously been dealt with in theology, and to encompass science within the same realm as artistic imagination, eventually ran into the sand. The scope of its inquiries and the ideas that informed them were lost, only to be revived by psychoanalysis a hundred years later. In the nineteenth century, physical science narrowed its definitions and moved rapidly within its own orbit, freed from the ball and chain of metaphysics. In Britain, first empirical, and then analytical, philosophy greatly increased precision by narrowing its focus and discarding metaphysics. In the resulting gap between science and philosophy, conventional religion reasserted itself. As John Stuart Mill put it in his essays on Jeremy Bentham (1838) and Coleridge (1840):

> the besetting danger is not so much of embracing falsehood for truth, as of mistaking part of the truth for the whole. It might be plausibly maintained that in almost every one of the leading controversies, past or present, in social philosophy, both sides were in the right in what they affirmed, though wrong in what they denied. [Leavis, 1950, p. 105]

This text can be applied to many fields of thought, and I think it is the case with dynamic and organic psychiatry, "both sides in the right in what they affirmed though wrong in what they denied". I would like to suggest that an approach to the middle ground inevitably comes from one or other end of the physical–mental axis.

Since we are at our best at either end of this axis, perhaps we should concentrate on refining our own area and be alert to what goes on the other side of the divide, in case a bridging point turns up. I have some hopes of one some day: that what I call the ego-function of belief might be seen at its work in some particular pattern of brain operation. Speaking from my psychoanalytic end, I have suggested that belief is an ego function that confers the status of conviction on mental content; that is, it treats phantasy as fact until proved otherwise, and that it confers on perceptions the status of "reality" (Britton, 1995). In my scheme of things, belief precedes reality testing, but, one hopes, remains open to it. It was the realization that this ordinary function could be lost that made me fully aware of its vital role in our lives, as we rely on it for our security, since we are frequently not in a position to know things for certain, such as the exact whereabouts and state of our loved ones. We live in a personal world of probability, and the physicists, since the 1920s, have shown us that so does the universe; uncertainty is what certainty was, and the sums of science add up to probability. So, we rely for our peace of mind on an ability to treat probability as certainty and belief as knowledge. This has always had a biological feel to it for me, and I would not be surprised if someday a corresponding physical link can be shown between one part of the brain and another that confers this property on mental content, similar to the way it is suggested that memory gains emotional significance. Here, I am clearly offering an amateur's approach, and my hope of gaining credibility requires me to return to my professional end of the axis.

Whatever neural system might underlie this belief function, it produces the touchstone of psychoanalysis, psychic reality. This can be our curse as well as our blessing. Descartes began his first philosophical meditation by saying

> Some years ago I was struck by the large number of falsehoods that I had accepted as true in my childhood, and by the doubtful nature of the whole edifice that I had subsequently based on them. [Ayer & O'Grady, 1992, p. 111]

Which of us could not say the same, and they do not die easily, these redundant beliefs, persisting often as unconscious sources of anxiety and depression. Indeed, uncovering them when they are repressed is the usual fare of analysis. However, the trouble unconscious beliefs cause is as nothing in comparison with the consequences when the function of belief itself is disordered.

What it is like to lose the capacity to believe without perceptual confirmation, to be unable to accept probability for knowledge, I have learnt from a number of cases. The resulting states are not simple, as they are accompanied by desperate efforts to mount delusional substitutes, much as Freud describes Schreber producing a delusional reconstruction as an attempt at recovery (Freud, 1911c, pp. 70–71).

Miss A was one such patient; she could not hold to the distinction between belief and knowledge. She could not derive any security from belief unless she could claim it as knowledge: *probability* did not exist for her only *possibility* or *certainty*. Unless, therefore, she believed she *knew* her object's exact whereabouts, she was in a panic. For this reason she developed elaborate strategies to avoid any occasion that would prompt her to doubt for a moment that she knew the whereabouts of her primary objects. This meant not only manipulating her environment, but also her mind. She was compelled by threats from within herself to empty her mind of the thoughts she was having. She did this by repeatedly flushing them down the lavatory. Another was trying to leave them behind in her flat and take to the streets. She had, however, to embark and re-embark many times to ensure she left her doubts behind. She was also a refugee from her ideas, as any possibility might gain the status of certainty unless she could rid herself of it. Possibility could arbitrarily mean certainty, just as probability, since it was not certainty, meant nothing.

Her ultimate weapon against uncertainty was a system of counter-beliefs, which she then treated as knowledge. These counter-beliefs in turn plagued her, as they had dire consequences. One such counter-belief was that she would go blind. From child-hood, her greatest fear was the fate of her mother if she was *out of sight*. Her mother's continuing existence *out of sight* meant she was *in the other room*. The *other room* was her parent's room, the setting of the primal scene, which, for this patient, was a murderous scenario. The counter-belief she mounted as protection from her own phan-tasy was that her mother was not out of sight, but that she herself was blind. This then became the belief that unless she saw her mother she would go blind. Finally, it took the form of "if my mother dies I will go blind". This was the form in which it emerged in the transference when she believed that my disappearance would cause her blindness. The only method of ridding herself of this belief was to take a number of physical actions representing evacuation of her mind symbolically, such as flushing the toilet repeatedly. She was a wealthy lady, and so functioned as a bag lady in a Mercedes, which contained most of her possessions to delay her return to her dreaded apartment, the container of her abandoned ideas.

There were many things about this case that relate to the ques-tion of what is psychic and what material, as Miss A endowed her thoughts with physical effects and various objects with super-natural significance. Mementos such as photographs, that com-monly commemorate emotionally significant events in physical form, had far more startling qualities for her. If anyone should by chance have included her in a photograph, she was convinced she would be trapped in the image and may be imprisoned in some stranger's drawer. As with everything else, such an idea necessitated action and avoidance.

What I am describing is Miss A living in a material world impregnated with ideas, and having a mind containing material objects. She had, at one stage, implored a surgeon to remove something solid from her mind, and was at one time at risk of being treated by psychosurgery; on the other hand, she believed that if she secretly took water from the tap in my bathroom and treated it like holy water, it would keep evil thoughts away.

One could say, in Gilbert Ryle's terms, that she was incessantly making category mistakes. But then, although we may not do so on the scale of Miss A, don't we all? Don't we treasure some physical objects and feel repulsed by others? Don't we feel guilty for thinking ill of someone even though we have taken no action? Human beings appear to create models of their own minds; models that, subject to linguistic analysis, may be as foolish or irrational as a belief in the ghost in the machine. Yet, the ghost self continues to haunt its bodily habitation and to have the company of other ghosts in its "erroneously" conceived inner space. We do not, at our best, think we have the bodies of our ancestors inside us, but our phantasies can have a solid sense to them, and, if we regress to psychotic states, we might revert to equating the idea of x with the body of x.

I am suggesting that believing is something we do from birth, like breathing. We treat our initial beliefs as facts and only begin to emancipate ourselves from them when first we realize that they are beliefs and not facts, and then question their validity. To realize that we believe rather than know something, we have to observe ourselves in the act of believing, to see ourselves relating to something and to see to what we are relating. To do that we have to have triangular space and a third position from which we can observe ourselves while being ourselves. In other words, to be what Coleridge called self-conscious, that is, as he put it, "Having consciousness of one's identity. One's actions, sensations, etc., reflectively aware of one's actions" (Coburn, 1974, p. 1).

As analysts, we deal with how people think, not how they should think, and we are aware that the relinquishment of one basic belief is as big a task as relinquishing an important object relationship. The process of giving up ideas because they prove to be unsatisfactory can be deceptive. In his paper *Das Unheimlich, The "Uncanny"* (1919h), in which he describes individuals having sudden eerie experiences, Freud distinguishes between *archaic beliefs*, which he sees as *surmounted* (*Überwundene*: outgrown, overcome, conquered, vanquished), but capable of re-emerging, from those which have been abolished. He wrote, "Anyone who has completely and finally rid himself [*Die Aufhebung des Glaubens*: the abolition of beliefs] of animistic beliefs will be insensible to this type of the *Unheimlich*" (Freud, 1919h, p. 248). I think this distinction is a most important one in analysis. I would make the distinction between beliefs that have merely been *surmounted* and those that have been worked through and *relinquished*. It is relinquishment that is necessary for psychic change, and it takes time, working through, and involves mourning for a lost belief like mourning a lost object. A belief that has been surmounted (*überwundene*) I regard as simply overlaid by another belief, and its quiescence remains dependent on the prevailing context of rationality and the authority of a parental transference figure; the surmounted belief, meanwhile, bides its time. It is like believing one thing when in company in daylight and another when alone in the dark. It is those lurking beliefs of the night that most interest us as analysts, those ghosts that vanish when we subject ourselves to the sharply focused light of educated reason. In contrast to the attempt to overcome beliefs that I take to characterize CBT, the aim of analysis is to find the hidden beliefs of our patients and to help them to relinquish them. In Freud's language, this would be *die Aufhebung des Glaubens*, the abolition of beliefs. I do not think, however, that it is the idea that is abolished when the link of belief is relinquished, any more than it is a person who is eradicated when the link to them of love or hate is given up. It is the link of belief that is abolished. Yet, all of us who practise analysis know how hard it is, and how long it takes, to give up love, hate, or belief.

References

Ayer, A. J., & O'Grady, J. (1992). *A Dictionary of Philosophical Quotations.* London: Blackwell.

Braithwaite, R. B. (1946). *Scientific Explanation*. Cambridge University Press, 1968.

Britton, R. (1995). Psychic reality and unconscious belief. *International Journal of Psychoanalysis*, 76(1): 19–23.

Coburn, K. (1951). *Inquiring Spirit*. London: Routledge & Kegan Paul.

Coburn, K. (1961). *The Notebooks of Samuel Taylor Coleridge*. New Haven, CT: Princeton University Press.

Coburn, K. (1974). *The Self-Conscious Imagination*. London: Oxford University Press.

Flew, A. (1979). *A Dictionary of Philosophy*. London: Macmillan.

Freud, S. (1895). Project for a Scientific Psychology. *S.E., I*. London: Hogarth.

Freud, S. (1911c). Psycho-analytic notes on an autobiographical account of a case of paranoia. *S.E., XI*: 3–84. London: Hogarth.

Freud, S. (1919h). The Uncanny. *S.E., XVII*. London: Hogarth.

Keynes, G. (1959). *Blake Complete Writings*. G. Keynes (Ed.). Oxford University Press.

Leavis, F. R. (1950). *Mill on Bentham and Coleridge*. F. R. Leavis (Ed.). Cambridge: Cambridge University Press.

Massicote, W. J. (1995). The surprising philosophical complexity of psychoanalysis (belatedly acknowledged). *Psychoanalytic & Contemporary Thought*, 18(1): 3–31.

Murdoch, I. (1977). *The Fire and the Sun*. London: Chatto and Windus.

Ryle, G. (1949). *The Concept of Mind*. London: Penguin.

CHAPTER TWO

Discussion of Ronald Britton's chapter on mind and matter

Leon Kleimberg

Reading Dr Britton's title of his chapter, "Mind and matter", and thinking about his doubts about the usefulness of polarizing mind and body, a fragment of a poem written by Marion Milner (2001) a psychoanalyst and an artist, came to my mind:

A language game

"What is mind? No matter"
"What is matter? Never mind." Who said this?

"Mind the gap!" Shouts the mechanical voice at the
   Embankment tube station.
"Mind the gap"
I do, I did, I never have fallen between the platform and the train.
I don't mind, it doesn't matter.
Or does it? . . .
I do mind the gap between the rich and the poor.
And I do mind the gap between what I can dream of for the earth
And what we are doing to it.
Destroying the living matter on which we depend for life—
like the Amazon Forests

And I mind that I did not think
It mattered that I did not mind
When we came to the
End of the matter.
So that there were
No more gaps
To mind.

Body and Mind, two sides of the same coin you said?

I minded that I did not mind
That the matter did not matter any more
But I do know that it is
Out of the gaps
That new things grow.

[Steiner & Johns, 2001]

Two thousand five hundred years ago, the Greek physician Hippocrates (460 BC) had a similar opinion to Dr Britton and Marion Milner regarding this particular point. He was quoted as saying, "Perhaps it is more important to know what sort of person has a disease than to know what sort of disease a person has".

Dr Britton states that the history of the development of the contradictions in science, philosophy, and the arts has lead to a polarization in understanding the connections between mind and body. In this brief discussion I will concentrate on what Dr Britton describes as the "middle ground" between the physical–mental axis and the very important experience of belief, and the ego-function of belief as one of the most important cornerstones in the creation and development of the mind and any further future links between mind and matter (Kleimberg, 2002).

But let us go back to Dr Britton's middle ground. I do agree with him in his view that this might be the starting point of what we call a mind. But first, in order to be able to comment further on this point, I quote what Freud says about the connections between mind and matter in his paper "Psychical (or mental) treatment" (1890a).

The affects in the narrower sense are, it is true, characterized by a quite special connection with somatic processes; but, strictly speaking, all mental states, including those that we usually regard as "processes of thought", are to some degree "affective", and not one of them is without its physical manifestations or is incapable of modifying somatic processes. Even when a person is engaged in quietly thinking in a string of "ideas", there are a constant series of excitations, corresponding to the content of these ideas, which are discharged into the smooth or striated muscles. These excitations can be made apparent if they are appropriately reinforced, and certain striking and, indeed, ostensibly "supernatural" phenomena can be explained by this means. [p. 288]

In terms of psychosexual human development, I believe, like Dr Britton, that mind and its corresponding intellectual and emotional processes start from birth, if not earlier. I have no doubt as well that belief as a form of *proto-knowledge* is also there from the beginning. However, this form of *proto-knowledge* that Dr Britton identifies as belief, cannot be isolated from its correspondent affective and emotional counterpart in the process of psychological birth and development, or in the continuous process of linking mind with body. As Freud's quote suggests, any psychosomatic link, as much as any link between a self and the other, or, for that matter, the baby and his mother, cannot happen outside the context and the realm of the affective or emotional response. Affects are not only the vehicle of communication between one and the other, but also between the mind and the body.

When Dr Britton describes the importance of belief and uncertainty as a forerunner to knowledge and to further psychological development or to its opposite results, he is describing only one aspect of the experience that gives birth to the mind and its links with the body. I believe, as Freud suggested in the quote above, that the other important aspect in the process that gives birth to the mind and keeps its links with the body and the object is the affective or emotional experience.

Winnicott (1951) describes this experience of psychic birth, as the process of illusionment and disillusionment in the journey towards separating the subject from the object (baby–mother). The process of successfully separating from the object, internalizing it, and developing a symbolic function (Segal 1991) based on such identification, is the cornerstone of the development of an internal world and of the experience that we describe as the mind. Being able to successfully separate from the object, in what Winnicott (1951) described as the process of disillusionment, can only happen if a relative period of sustaining an illusion of being one and the same with the object is allowed and tolerated. Being successful in negotiating separation and disillusionment from the primary identification with the object will, one hopes, lead towards the development of the experience of the transitional phenomena, a true cornerstone for psychological development and individuation.

Marion Milner (1952) has described a similar experience and process in what she describes as the role of illusion in symbol formation; that is, the need to be one with the other before we can truly develop a genuine sense of ourselves. When Dr Britton describes psychological struggles between probability and certainty and belief and knowledge, I believe it does not happen in a vacuum. It is happening in the context of an emotional relationship.

Miss A's struggles with belief and disbelief are happening in the context of anxieties and murderous feelings towards threats of separation, separateness, and abandonment. As Freud suggests, the link between the development of Miss A's mind as separated from her body and the development of herself as a person, separated and different from her mother or from Dr Britton, depends on the affective responses towards separation anxieties and on the creation of a mind that can tolerate boundaries and separation from the other.

This process, or struggle, it is my impression, is as much an emotional one as one of developing and sorting out ideas and beliefs. It is difficult to know which one comes first or how they interact with each other. But I believe they are inseparable: belief and emotion, belief and illusion.

The connection between mind and body and the emergence of the mind as a sort of "virtual or telescopic experience" is the result of the constant dialectic interaction between these two aspects of human development. In terms of Winnicott, what gives birth to a mind and keeps its connection to the body is how a baby negotiates his separateness from the mother. It is an emotional struggle between wanting to keep the illusion of being fused with the mother and having to accept and tolerate the disillusionment of the impossibility of such a reality and mental state. On the whole, we never really resolve this illusion of wanting to be reunited fully with the mother. This is the stuff of what dreams are made of, as well as of religion, arts, or even sports. Unsuccessful negotiations in this area of disillusionment and separateness bring psychopathology in the personal and social arena.

In the dialectic interaction between illusion and belief in this early area of development is where mind as a virtual and symbolic experience is born. The area of illusion and belief is also where the connection between the mind and the body exists, and remains. The area of illusion and belief is where ultimately creativity and pathology begins. The working through of its different complexities, which needs to be done in this area in order to achieve psychic change and personal development, is not only in the area of knowledge, belief, and ideas, but also in the area of illusion, rage, guilt, grief, chaos, conflict, hopelessness, and pain (Kleimberg, 2006).

A patient of mine, Mr D, suffered from continuous physical ailments; liver pain, stomach pain, bleeding from the digestive system, but never found a medical justification for those painful states. He had no choice but to accept that the problem was in his mind. Realizing such a state of affairs was a very painful and disturbing experience to undertake. Years of not using his mind, or not having a mind to use, left so much damage behind him to himself and his family that the pain and guilt he had to endure to own this knowledge was very difficult for him and for his analyst. He had an appalling childhood background, his children were also developing psychosomatic illnesses, and a large part of his life had been wasted by other tragic events.

In terms of Dr Britton's (1995) systems of belief and disbelief, Mr D's systems of belief and disbelief were geared not to see, or to see only the positive. We had to struggle against the emotional pain, guilt, and chaos that challenging the system of belief and disbelief brought with it.

Mr D persisted with the illusion of being one and the same person with an idealized mother in phantasy, because the guilt and psychic pain and chaos of letting this belief–disbelief go when separating from this idealized mother was too overwhelming and disintegrating an experience for him. Ultimately, what felt like an insurmountable barrier for Mr D was to have to develop a mind that could take and contain so much pain, guilt, and chaos.

The emotional need to maintain the "illusion of being fused in phantasy with a perfect mother that one day is going to make everything fine" becomes a resilient defence and a deceitful system of belief and knowledge necessary for him to protect himself from unbearable psychic pain. At the moment, for Mr D, letting his liver carry the pain seems a better solution and belief than letting go of the protective blissful illusion. For Mr D, letting the idealized object go entails having to endure the birth of a mind that comes with a very painful burden.

In conclusion, it is the birth of the mind and its continuous links with the body which occurs in the primary area of illusion and belief.

Illusion is the emotional component that contains the experience of separateness and union with the mother, and, as Dr Britton suggests, belief–disbelief is the ego-function that contains the emotional–intellectual experience in the form of *proto-knowledge*, or the early process of *proto-thinking*.

Dr Britton's concept of belief and knowledge operates as an integral part of the area of separation and disillusionment with the object, as two sides of the same developmental spectrum. Successful working through in this particular spectrum of illusion and belief should eventually lead to the development of people with a good enough degree of maturity, integration, psychic mobility, and sense of reality. Yet, as Dr Britton suggested in his chapter, in a similar way, belief and knowledge in the form of disbelief or certainty can also be used to avoid processes of disillusionment.

Another way of understanding belief in this emotional frame could be as a proto-concept that operates in the threshold between illusion and disillusionment, helping in this way to keep the connection between phantasy, desire, and knowledge. A good example of this would be a patient who, at times of crisis or breakdown, loses belief in his capacity to live, but is kept alive by the illusion that somebody will come and help. Or the reverse situation, where the same patient becomes disillusioned with life but believes that things will get better or someone will come and help him stay alive. The worst scenario in this type of situation would be when misfortune strikes, and disillusionment with the object and life coincides with the belief that there is no one that will come and help.

It is also implied in this discussion that separateness, as well as the system of belief and uncertainty, is an experience needing to be negotiated constantly in the level of dual personal relationships and the level of the triangular personal relationships. The successful or unsuccessful way this two-way system experience is negotiated in the epigenetic process of development (Erikson, 1968) will generate a symbolic and virtual experience described as the mind. Creativity, in its many forms, such as art, religion, or civilization also derives from this, as well as pathology and social malaise.

In his paper on psychic treatment, Freud was also very clear in his belief that this early, intertwined area of the mind and body could be also influenced by the "magic of words" (1890a), via the suggestive influence of the emotional relationship that is the transference. Perhaps now, one hundred years later, we know that this area can also be influenced and stimulated by many other internal or external experiences, other than just the "magical words".

We know now that any affective or sensorial experience like the arts, music, hypnosis, meditation, or religious faith has the potential to stimulate and connect the mind with the body in a way that can affect each other significantly.

Finally, to end this discussion on a simpler note, let me tell you that in my research for information on this theme, I asked a few adolescents about these matters, in search for some answers to this obscure problem. After all, adolescents are supposed to be in the middle of these existential struggles between mind and body.

I asked a sixteen-year-old boy what he thought of the relation between his mind and his body and what did he feel was more important to him, his mind or his body? After some tribulations, this young man's simple but passionate answer was, "What kind of a question is that . . . I don't know . . . it is like asking me who is more important, my mother or my father! They are actually both equally important to me in their own way! Each of them does something important . . . Mum does the looking after . . . dad helps with the discipline!"

This statement perhaps indicates that the links within the spectrum of mind and matter also involve an aspect of human experience that has to do with the internalization of a parental couple that is capable of connecting physically and emotionally with the child and between themselves.

References

Britton, R. (1995). Psychic reality and unconscious belief. *International Journal of the Psychoanalytic Association, 76*(1): 19–23.
Erikson, E. H. (1968). *Identity:Youth and Crisis.* London: Faber and Faber.

Freud, S. (1890a). Psychical (or mental) treatment. *S.E.*, *7*: 283–304. London: Hogarth.

Steiner, R., & Johns, J. (2001). *Within Time and Beyond Time.A Festschrift For Pearl King*. London: Karnac.

Kleimberg, L. (2002). Minding the gap, psychoanalysis and creativity ... and what about the space in between? *The Bulletin of the British Psychoanalytic Society*, *38*(6): 45–54.

Kleimberg, L. (2006). Some reflections on the connections between aggression and depression. In: C. Harding (Ed.), *Aggression and Destructiveness: Psychoanalytic Perspectives* (pp. 181–193). London: Routledge.

Milner, M. (1952). The role of illusion in symbol formation. In: *The Suppressed Madness of Sane Men*. London: The New Library of Psychoanalysis, 1987.

Segal, H. (1991). *Dream, Phantasy and Art*. London: The New Library of Psychoanalysis.

Winnicott, D. W. (1951). Transitional objects and transitional phenomena. In: *Through Paediatrics to Psychoanalysis*. London: Hogarth, 1982.

CHAPTER THREE

Mechanisms of change in mentalization-based treatment of borderline personality disorder*

Peter Fonagy and Anthony W. Bateman

There are very few less contentious issues than the role of attachment in psychotherapy. Concepts such as the therapeutic alliance speak directly to the importance of activating the attachment system, normally in relation to the therapist in individual therapy and in relation to other family members in family-based intervention, if therapeutic progress is to be made. In group therapy, the attachment process may be activated by group membership. The past decade of neuroscientific research has helped us to understand some key processes that attachment entails at brain level. This chapter outlines this progress and links it to recent findings on the relationship between the neural systems underpinning attachment and other processes such as making of social judgements, theory of mind, and access to long-term memory. These findings allow intriguing speculations, which are currently undergoing empirical tests on the neural basis of individual differences in attachment as well as the nature of psychological disturbances

---

*This chapter was previously published in 2006 as a paper in *Journal of Clinical Psychology*, 62(4): 411–430

associated with profound disturbances of the attachment system. In this chapter, we explore the crucial paradoxical brain state created by psychotherapy with powerful clinical implications for the maximization of therapeutic benefit from the talking cure.

Overview

Borderline personality disorder (BPD) is a complex and serious mental disorder that is characterized by a pervasive pattern of difficulties with emotion regulation, impulse control, and instability both in relationships and in self-image, with a mortality rate, associated with suicide, that is fifty times that of the general population (Skodol, et al., 2002b).[1] The dysfunction of self-regulation is particularly apparent in the context of social relationships (e.g., Posner et al., 2002).

The regulation of emotion and the catastrophic reaction to the loss of intensely emotionally invested social ties together place borderline personality disorder in the domain of attachment. A number of theorists have drawn on Bowlby's ideas in explanation of borderline pathology (Holmes, 2003). Gunderson (1996) carefully described typical patterns of borderline dysfunction in terms of exaggerated reactions of the insecurely attached infant, for example, clinging, fearfulness about dependency needs, terror of abandonment, and constant monitoring of the proximity of the caregiver. Lyons-Ruth and Jacobovitz (1999) focused on the disorganization of the attachment system in infancy as predisposing to later borderline pathology. Crittenden (1997) has incorporated in her representation of adult attachment disorganization the specific style of BPD individuals who are deeply ambivalent about, and fearful of, close relationships. We (Fonagy, Target, & Gergely, 2000) have also used the framework of attachment theory, but emphasize the role of attachment in the development of symbolic function and the way in which insecure disorganized attachment might generate vulnerability in the face of further turmoil and challenges.

Further support for the central role of attachment in the disorder is found in the evidence that psychotherapy is the most effective treatment modality, although pharmacotherapy may enhance its effects. However, the mechanism of change remains unknown.

Given the strong suggestion of abnormal (disorganized) attachment processes and the consequent instability in emotions and relationships in BPD, we suggest that the mechanism mediating change indeed occurs via the improved regulation of neuropsychological systems underpinning the organization of interpersonal relationships (Bateman & Fonagy, 2004).

Mechanisms of change: causing change in causal mechanisms

Discussing the therapeutic action of psychotherapy with BPD patients assumes that psychotherapy is indeed therapeutic. Although evidence for this claim is gradually accumulating (Roth & Fonagy, 2005), we do not know how psychotherapy effects change, and, given the relatively rapid rate of spontaneous improvement (Zanarini, Frankenburg, Hennen, & Silk, 2003) in BPD, the observations of symptomatic improvements in uncontrolled studies should be considered with great caution. If we were to start from first principles, an understanding of the processes underpinning psychopathology would inform treatment innovation, which in turn would then be subject to empirical investigation. Kazdin (2004) has outlined a radical and rigorous programme for psychotherapy research based on these principles. The first stage follows from the proposition that treatment should reflect what we know about the processes that directly bear on the onset and course of a clinical problem. In Kazdin's model, demonstration that a specific process was present in a sizable proportion of individuals with a specific presentation would be the basis of treatment development. Further, rather than assuming that all individuals who have the same presentation would be equally responsive to treatment, further work would aim to detect subtypes of a dysfunction, multiple pathways to the same presentation, as well as risk and protective factors. The second step asks questions about the processes by which a treatment method achieves change, first by specifying the processes or factors responsible for change, then by developing measures of these processes, and finally by showing that these processes change before therapeutic change occurs. On this basis, manualization becomes feasible, on the presumption that the manual now includes a high dosage of "effective" ingredients.

Evaluation of outcome can then follow, along with process-outcome studies that aim to examine moderator variables (helping us to discover more about what actually does work for whom).

Following Kazdin's proposal, we shall first consider a comprehensive model of biological and psychosocial factors that are present together in BPD. Each of the components and the evidence associated with dysfunction in the domains specified are outlined. Second, we consider how the therapeutic technique we favour, mentalization-based treatment (MBT), links to components of the proposed mechanisms underlying the pathology of BPD. Finally, we offer preliminary (inevitably somewhat speculative) ideas as to how psychotherapeutic intervention *might* be seen to address these dysfunctions. In so doing, we consider psychotherapy more broadly than our own approach, as it is inherently unlikely that specific mechanisms exist for each of the therapeutic models apparently relatively successfully used in this clinical context.

BPD as a deficit in attachment-related mentalization

Our view of BPD and attachment has undergone a number of changes as a result of accumulating data. In 1989, we suggested that a better understanding of the features of borderline personality disorder could be achieved if we assumed that patients who had this diagnosis had a limited capacity to mentalize, that is, to comprehend and use their knowledge of their own and others' states of mind (Fonagy, 1989). Our original theory of mentalization dysfunction suggested that the apparent inability to process mental states effectively and appropriately in an attachment context was a defensive reaction to physical or sexual abuse, which led to a decoupling of mental processes underpinning thinking about feelings and thoughts in self and others (Fonagy, 1991). Later on, we added that constitutional factors were also likely to be involved (Bateman & Fonagy, 2004).

Building on accumulating evidence from developmental psychopathology, the mentalization theory of borderline personality disorder suggests that individuals either constitutionally vulnerable (Torgersen et al., 2000) and/or exposed to neglect in early relationships (Battle et al., 2004) in which their emotional experience is not adequately mirrored by the care-giver (Crandell, Patrick, & Hobson, 2003) develop with an enfeebled or fragile capacity to represent affect and effortfully control their attentional capacities (Posner et al., 2002). When confronted with trauma (Battle et al., 2004), these individuals are more likely to react by decoupling their capacity to deal with their own or others' mental states comprehensively, particularly in an attachment context (Fonagy et al., 1996). We may think of this decoupling as adaptive, a deliberate avoidance of the state of mind of the perpetrator of maltreatment. The child cannot be expected to accept fully what must be the frankly hostile intentional stance of the abuser. It may be easier not to think about mental states as a whole. There may be more to this than an adaptation. Early trauma may cause changes in the neural mechanisms of arousal that lead to a relatively ready triggering of the arousal system underpinning posterior cortical activation while taking the frontal mentalizing parts of the brain "offline" in response to relatively mild emotional stimuli (Arnsten, 1998).

Whatever the immediate cause of the decoupling, its consequence is the re-emergence of modes of thinking about internal states that antedate the fully fledged mentalizing capacity of the adult. In previous work, we discussed three of these that we claim are relatively readily observable in typical patterns of thinking of individuals who have BPD: the psychic equivalent, the pretend, and the teleological mode of representing the internal world (Fonagy, Gergely, Jurist, & Target, 2002). All these are modes of representing subjectivity that developmentally antedate the emergence of full mentalization (Flavell & Miller, 1998; Gopnik, 1993). Children of two or three years of age tend to assume a direct correspondence between what is in their mind and what is physically true. A small child's unshakable belief that there is a tiger under the bed is an example of psychic equivalence. At other times children can contemplate an internal reality as long as no connection is made to the real world, as in early pretend play. While psychic equivalence makes subjective experience too real, the pretend mode severs its connection with reality and, at an extreme, is tantamount to dissociation. Finally, the teleological mode refers to a unique dependence on what is observable in thinking about intentions. Often, individuals who have BPD seek proof in physical action as part of a full confirmation of a subjective state. For example, one is being loved only if one is physically touched.

Within our theoretical frame of reference, dysfunctional attachment relationships not only are the consequence of the difficulty in holding a stable and consistent representation of others' and one's own mind in mind (Liotti, 2002), but also cause developmental distortions in self-organization. We have suggested a model that might explain this striking sequence. Representations of emotions cannot emerge without interaction with another person, who mirrors the infant's experience and whose reflections of this experience are internalized by the infant. When the care-giver's mirroring is not congruent, the infant organizes internal experience by internalizing the care-giver, rather than the care-giver's mirroring the child, as suggested by Winnicott (1956). Thus, such second-order representations of internal states are, by definition, "alien". They do not match the constitutional state of the self. Consequently, the self-organization evolves in a somewhat flawed manner.

A further factor, trauma, contributes to the foregrounding of self-fragmentation (identity diffusion) in BPD. We suggest that traumatized individuals can use discontinuities within the self—in other words, the alien parts of the self—to adapt to incomprehensible assault from someone connected to them by attachment bonds by "identifying with the aggressor" (Freud, 1936). The tragic consequence of this manner of self-protection is the modification of self-organization, so that the self now incorporates the abusive intention. This modification generates momentary experiences of unbearable psychic pain when the self feels attacked literally from within and almost overwhelmed by an experience of "badness", which is hardly mitigated by reassurance. Experienced in the mode of psychic equivalence, the feeling of badness translates directly into "actual badness", from which self-destruction might appear the only escape. In our view, this state is commonly the trigger for acts of self-harm and suicide.

In summary we are proposing that a constitutionally vulnerable individual who experiences developmental trauma in an attachment context becomes psychologically vulnerable in later attachment contexts as a result of instability of the self. In an attempt to cope, the individual decouples the mind from others' minds and relies on earlier psychological mechanisms to organize the experience, and in doing so reveals fragments of the self.

If our suggestions are correct, the enhancement of mentalization and the reduction of the predominance of non-mentalizing modes of experiencing internal reality represent the path to cure.

The nature of the therapeutic intervention and the process of change

Although there have been several attempts to describe mentalization-focused therapy from a psychoanalytic standpoint for children (e.g., Bleiberg, Fonagy, & Target, 1997) and adults (e.g., Fonagy, Gergely, Jurist, & Target, 2002), the first comprehensive description of the therapeutic approach is to be found in Bateman and Fonagy's description of the partial hospital-based treatment of BPD (see Bateman & Fonagy, 2004). There is limited but good-quality evidence for the effectiveness of the approach (Bateman & Fonagy, 1999, 2001, 2003) with further studies under way. We believe that psychotherapy has the potential to recreate an interactional matrix of attachments in which mentalization develops and flourishes. The therapist's mentalizing in a way that fosters the patient's mentalizing is seen as a critical facet of the therapeutic relationship and the essence of the mechanism of change. The crux of the value of psychotherapy is the experience of another human being's having the patient's mind in mind.

The key features of this psychotherapeutic approach may be summarized as follows.

1. The therapist is asked exclusively to focus on patients' current mental state (their thoughts, feelings, wishes, and desires) with the aim of building up representations of internal states.
2. The therapist is asked to avoid situations in which the patient talks of mental states that he or she cannot link to subjectively felt reality. Thus, there is deviation from traditional psychodynamic technique in that
    (a) there is a de-emphasis of "deep" unconscious concerns in favour of conscious or near-conscious content and less focus on the past as it is represented in the present;

(b) the aim of therapy is not insight but the recovery of mentalization: achieving representational coherence and integration for intentional states;

(c) the therapist avoids describing complex mental states (such as conflict, ambivalence, unconscious) and is asked to make "small interpretations" referring to ideation that is only slightly beyond the boundaries of the patient's conscious thinking.

3. In this way, the therapy creates a transitional area of relatedness in which thoughts and emotions can be "played with."

4. The inevitable enactments over the course of the treatment are not interpreted or understood in terms of their unconscious meaning but in terms of the situation and affects immediately before the enactment.

For a fuller discussion of the key features of MBT and its similarities with, and differences from, other therapeutic approaches, see Bateman and Fonagy (2004).

The biological basis of therapeutic change in MBT

The role of neuroscience in psychological therapies

Returning to our original contention that change results from improvement in regulation of neuropsychological systems, we must consider the biological basis of the change caused by the therapeutic approach outlined. Although BPD is one of the most investigated of the personality disorders (PDs), its neurobiological basis is relatively unknown even though research is rapidly identifying neural correlates of complex subjective states (Adolphs, 2003), for example, concern about the mental states of another person (Frith & Frith, 2003). Natural recovery from BPD (Zanarini, Frankenburg, Hennen, & Silk, 2003), sometimes dramatic (Gunderson et al., 2003), and substantial treatment-related improvements (e.g., Linehan et al., 2002), suggest that the psychoneurobiological processes of BPD should relate to a reversible brain state rather than permanent abnormalities or alterations of function.

On the basis of the key dysfunctions of BPD, namely, impulsivity and interpersonal problems, there are two regions of brain function that link psychological processes of particular relevance to psychotherapy for BPD and biological processes: (1) reward circuits and attachment and (2) dysfunctions of interpersonal relatedness and mentalization. We shall briefly consider knowledge in these areas in turn and consider the links between them.

The biology of reward and attachment

Our suggestion is that the poor functioning of the reward system in individuals who have BPD is linked to the dysfunction of the attachment system by their shared neural basis.

Individuals who have BPD make "impulsive choices" that result in appetitive reward in the short term, but have the potential to be self-damaging in the long run. Examples of these choices include gambling, irresponsible spending, binge eating, substance abuse, unsafe sex, and reckless driving. These impulsive choices all require the individual to assign greater value to immediate, short-term reward than to long-term rewards such as safety and security. We may think of this kind of impulsivity as characterized by actions that are poorly conceived and prematurely expressed (Daruna & Barnes, 1993).

The simplest analogues of this type of impulsive behaviour have been investigated within laboratory studies (Rogers et al., 1999). Individuals who have BPD make poor estimations of likely outcomes in estimating the likelihood of monetary reward (Bazanis et al., 2002). The pattern of maladaptive performance was similar to that of individuals who had focal lesions to the orbitofrontal cortex (Rogers et al., 1999), a region previously associated with reward anticipation and valuation. A further study showed that BPD patients choose short-delay small rewards over longer-delay, larger rewards (Dougherty, Bjork, Huckabee, Moeller, & Swann, 1999). Recent animal work implicates the nucleus accumbens (Nac) in temporal bias towards short-term over long-term rewards (Cardinal, Pennicott, Sugathapala, Robbins, & Everitt, 2001). This, combined with the dopaminergic reward system of the Nac's being implicated in an animal model of impulsivity, suggests that the Nac specifically, and the mesencephalic dopaminergic reward system (MDRS) in general, might be involved in bias towards short-term reward and might be characteristic of the maladaptive valuation and decision making of individuals who have BPD.

The mesencephalic dopaminergic reward system has also been implicated in the process of drug addiction and the neurobiological process of attachment. The pathway of interest includes the ventral tegmental area (VTA), which projects directly and indirectly via the amygdala/bed nucleus of the stria terminalis to the nucleus accumbens. From here, projections are to the ventral pallidum and from there to the thalamus. The thalamic projections go to the prefrontal and cingulate cortex, which are thought to activate cells that ultimately feed back to the VTA (Everitt & Wolf, 2002). It appears that, broadly speaking, drugs that lead to dopamine release in this system, such as psychostimulants, are addictive (Koob & Le Moal, 1997), although the neurochemical basis of addiction and substance use is probably more complicated than dopamine release (Insel, 2003). Given that it is unlikely that nature created a brain system specifically to serve drug and alcohol abuse, it seems most likely that addiction is the accidental by-product of the activation of a biological system that plays a crucial evolutionary function. MacLean (1990) speculated that substance abuse and drug addiction were attempts to replace opiates or endogenous factors normally provided by social attachments. Similarly, Panksepp (1998) suggested a common neurobiological process of mother–infant, infant–mother, and male–female attachment relationships linked to the mesocorticolimbic dopaminergic reward circuit. More recently, Insel (2003) summarized relevant data that seem to answer in the affirmative the question, "Is social attachment an addictive disorder?"

There is good evidence, reviewed by Insel (2003), that mesocorticolimbic pathways also mediate mother–infant interactions in rats: (1) dopamine is released and c-Fos (a proto-oncogene that encodes a 55,000-molecular-weight phosphoprotein, Fos, which is thought to assist in the regulation of "target genes" containing an activating protein-1 [AP-1] binding site), is activated in the nucleus accumbens when maternal females are exposed to their pups (Stack, Balakrishnan, Numan, & Numan, 2002); (2) lesions of the VTA and the nucleus accumbens reduce the females' approach and interaction with pups (Lee, Li, Watchus, & Fleming, 1999); (3) cocaine or c-flupenthixol (a nonspecific dopamine antagonist) injected directly into the nucleus accumbens causes a decrease in pup retrieval (Vernotica, Rosenblatt, & Morrell, 1999); (4) Insel and his group demonstrated that the neuropeptides oxytocin (OT) and vasopressin (AVP) are released by sociosexual experience and may serve as an important link by which parturition, copulation, and lactation can activate this reward circuit, leading to the suggestion that OT and AVP activity marks the generic reward states as specifically attachment-related (Young, Lim, Gingrich, & Insel, 2001).

There is further good evidence that the mesocorticolimbic pathways also mediate pair bonding in rodents (Insel & Young, 2000). Prairie and pine voles form partner preferences and pair bonds after mating, whereas montane and meadow voles do not form selective attachments. Thus, it is of substantial interest that in prairie, but not montane, voles dopamine release in Nac is associated with mating (Gingrich, Liu, Cascio, Wang, & Insel, 2000) and that D2 (dopamine 2) receptor agonists infused into the Nac induce, and antagonists prevent, partner preferences (Wang et al., 1999). These and numerous other studies support the notion that mesolimbic dopamine activation of D2 receptors is necessary and sufficient for the development of a partner preference (in prairie voles). Vole research also suggests the hypothesis that mating releases OT and AVP, which amplify the dopamine signal in the Nac shell (Insel, 2003). We can add more recent evidence that the ventral pallidum, located within the ventral forebrain and part of the mesolimbic dopamine reward pathway, shows high density of vasopressin V1a receptors (V1aRs) in the monogamous prairie and pine voles, but not in the promiscuous meadow or montane voles (Lim, Murphy, & Young, 2004). Site-specific infusion of a selective V1aR antagonist into the ventral pallidum blocks pair bond formation in prairie voles (Lim & Young, 2004). Thus, V1aRs in the ventral forebrain appear to be crucial for pair bond formation, and this V1aR pattern seems to be correlated with monogamous social organization. Experimental evidence supporting this hypothesis is found in a single gene manipulation study (Lim et al., 2004). Partner preference formation (measured as time spent huddling with a partner as opposed to a stranger vole) in the socially promiscuous meadow vole could be increased by using viral vector V1aR gene transfer into the ventral forebrain. The over-expression of V1aR in the ventral pallidum leads to the development of partner preference in this interpersonally undiscriminating rodent. What we see here is a potential molecular mechanism for the rapid evolution of complex social behaviour and the possible recreation of a singular critical evolutionary event in the laboratory.

Knowledge from preclinical (animal) models is confirmed by neuroimaging studies that demonstrate an association between functional brain activity related to attachment and cortical and subcortical sites in the human brain that contain a high density of the neurohormones OT and AVP. Imaging shows that the mesocorticolimbic dopaminergic pathway is activated while processing attachment related stimuli. Strathearn and McClure (2002) studied the brain activation in mothers while viewing pictures of their own infants and compared it to the pattern of activation when they looked at infants who were familiar, but not their own, in three affective states (crying, smiling, and neutral expressions). They reported significant differences in the activation of the right globus pallidus–ventral striatum, the left putamen, the bed nucleus of the stria terminals, the nucleus accumbens, the amygdala, the bilateral hippocampi, and the fusiform face area (FFA). A very similar study (Nitschke et al., 2004) also reported activation in the orbitofrontal areas (OFC) in the mothers watching their own infants, which correlated with their hedonic mood state, which was also measured in the study. OFC activation is, of course, also observed in other studies in response to pleasant experiences: taste, smell, money, winning, positive feedback, nicotine, cocaine (Kawabata & Zeki, 2004). The most compelling recent study is that of Bartels and Zeki (2004), who, using the contrast of own *vs.* other child, controlled for age and familiarity, were able to demonstrate activity in the substantia nigra, globus pallidus, subthalamic nuclei, bed nucleus of the stria terminalis, and ventral tegmental area, constituting almost all of the regions critical for the attachment-mediating neuropeptides in the human brain. As these workers had already reported a functional magnetic resonance imaging (fMRI) study of romantic love using a similar contrast design (Bartels & Zeki, 2000), they were able to confirm that most of the regions activated by maternal love were the same as those that they had found to be associated with romantic love, that is, those in the striatum (the putamen, globus pallidus, caudate nucleus), the middle insula, and the dorsal part of the cingulate cortex.

In summary it has been established that mesocorticolimbic dopamine is an important candidate in the mediation of reward, the capacity for deferred gratification, and addiction, but is also critical for maternal behaviour in rats and pair bonding in voles. A circuit linking a vasopressin-sensitive mechanism within the anterior hypothalamus (medial preoptic area [MPOA]) to the VTA and the nucleus accumbens shell may be especially important for mediating the rewarding properties of social interaction, which are dysfunctional in BPD patients in line with their difficulties in forming normal attachments. The neuropeptides OT and AVP are released by sociosexual experience in rodents and humans. When we activate this reward circuit, a change in attachment behaviour follows (at least in voles). fMRI studies indicate activation of same pathways in response to stimuli relating to the participant's own infant and partner. We may conclude that a major neural system underpinning attachment has been identified.

Dysfunctional interpersonal relatedness and a deficit in mentalization

Disturbed interpersonal relatedness has also been identified as a key aspect of BPD relative to other PDs (e.g., Skodol et al., 2002a). This aspect can refer to a range of difficulties, including dramatic shifts from idealization of to disillusionment with others, frantic efforts to prevent perceived abandonment, and inappropriate interpersonal aggression. However, an emerging literature suggests that all of these may share common mechanistic and aetiologic features. Specifically, disorganized attachment in the relationships of individuals who have BPD may mediate the expression of interpersonal problems among individuals. Individuals who have BPD have a model of relationships characterized by insecurity of attachment relative to other groups of Axis I or Axis II patients (e.g., Barone, 2003). On numerous measures of adult attachment, patients who have BPD are identified as insecure, preoccupied, and fearful in their relationships (e.g., Patrick, Hobson, Castle, Howard, & Maughan, 1994). Patients who have BPD have been characterized as having a specific type of disorganized, anxious–preoccupied attachment focused around an approach–avoidance dilemma in which the attachment figure is simultaneously perceived as a source of threat and a secure base (Crandell, Patrick, & Hobson, 2003). A variety of lines of research suggest that the disordered attachment that is characteristic of BPD results from psychosocial experiences of maltreatment (e.g., Trull, 2001) and premorbid temperamental attributes of negative affectivity and aggressive impulsivity (e.g., Silk, 2000). Surprisingly, although there is strong evidence for both the psychosocial mechanism (abnormal attachment) and psychosocial cause (maltreatment) of interpersonal difficulties in BPD (e.g., Skodol et al., 2002c), a neurobiological account of disrupted interpersonal interactions remains elusive. Explorations of the subscales of a self-report measure of interpersonal relatedness identified two types of problems experienced by BPD patients: one group have difficulty in achieving closeness to others and another group feel extremely submissive, unable to state needs, and avoidant of conflict (Leihener et al., 2003). At least the problems of the first group might be related to a deficit of social cognition that makes accurate perception of the respective mental states of self and other and self–other differentiation difficult (Fonagy, Target, & Gergely, 2000). Deficits of this aspect of interpersonal perception have been demonstrated in analogue studies using film clips (e.g., Arntz & Veen, 2001), affect recognition and alexithymic symptoms (e.g., Sayar, Ebrinc, & Ak, 2001), and narratives of childhood experience (Fonagy et al., 1996).

A deficit of interpersonal awareness implies an underlying failure to distinguish clearly between one's own and others' mental states. Some of the brain abnormalities identified in borderline patients are consistent with the suggestion that a failure of representation of self-states is a key dysfunction. Some evidence suggests that the anterior cingulate cortex plays a key role in mentalizing the self, at least in the domain of emotional states (Frith & Frith, 2003). Lane has proposed more specifically that implicit self-representations (i.e., phenomenal self-awareness) can be localized to the dorsal anterior cingulate, whereas explicit self-representations (i.e., reflection) can be localized to the rostral anterior cingulate (Lane, 2000). Activation of the medial prefrontal cortex has been demonstrated in a series of neuroimaging studies in conjunction with a wide range of mentalization inferences, in both visual and verbal domains (Gallagher et al., 2000). It appears that the prefrontal cortex is involved when mentalizing interactively in a way that requires implicitly representing the mental states of others. The mesial prefrontal cortex, the parietotemporal junction, and the temporal poles constitute a network of areas that are invariably active when mentalizing activity is taking place (Gallagher & Frith, 2003). The same area of the brain is involved in other tasks that have been clinically described as challenging to patients who have borderline personality problems, including assessing social trustworthiness (Winston, Strange, O'Doherty, & Dolan, 2002), interpreting the meaning of facial expressions (Critchley et al., 2000), making moral judgements (Greene & Haidt, 2002), and performing tasks that entail attending to one's own emotions (Gusnard, Akbudak, Shulman, & Raichle, 2001). It has been argued that exposure to stress impairs prefrontal cortical function and the impairment may be catecholamine mediated (Arnsten, 1998). In line with this suggestion is the observation that the concentration of N-acetyl-aspartate (NAA), a marker of neural integrity, is lowered in the anterior cingulated region of the medial prefrontal cortex of maltreated children and adolescents (De Bellis, Keshavan, Spencer, & Hall, 2000).

The loose coupling of attachment and mentalization

So far, we have described two systems in which borderline functional deficits are evident, certainly at the behavioural level and, on preliminary neurobiological evidence, at the biological level. First, the mesolimbic dopaminergic reward system underpinning attachment might be dysfunctional in BPD. This dysfunction is suggested both by the poor ability of individuals who have BPD to delay gratification and the evident disorganization of their attachment system. The overlapping neural underpinnings of these deficits might suggest that therapeutically addressing either set of issues may indirectly benefit the other. Thus, behavioural approaches, such as dialectical behaviour therapy (DBT), which begin by addressing the reward systems in general and impulsivity in particular, might, through such interventions, also have an impact on the quality of functioning within the attachment system (although it was not part of the original aim of DBT). Equally, the possibility of a common deficit underpinning these two aspects of BPD dysfunction might explain the beneficial effects that improvements in attachment relationships might generate for problems of impulsivity or decision making.

Second, the mesial prefrontal cortex, the parietotemporal junction, and the temporal poles are related to the deficits in mentalization in interpersonal interactions. The suggestion here is that a focus on mentalization addresses some of the social cognitive dysfunctions that generate inappropriate behaviour in BPD, particularly suspiciousness, aggression, insensitivity to social situations, and inadequate capacity to focus attention on self-states to a degree pertinent to the interaction.

Attachment and mentalization systems are probably not independent of each other but in subtle ways might be "loosely coupled". This suggestion is based on the finding that securely attached children are relatively precocious in the development of mentalization (Fonagy, Steele, Steele, & Holder, 1997; Meins, Fernyhough, Russel, & Clark-Carter, 1998) and the quality of parental mentalization of a child facilitates the development of secure attachment (Fonagy, Steele, Moran, Steele, & Higgitt, 1991). More recently, the intersection of mentalization capacity and social experience has been more generally noted (Carpendale & Lewis, 2004), although the specific nature of the interface remains controversial.

Increased understanding of the neural mechanisms underpinning attachment may provide a further important clue. As previously mentioned, Bartels and Zeki (2000, 2004), in two separate studies, reported that maternal and romantic attachment appeared systematically to suppress brain activity in regions associated with emotionally charged memories, negative emotions, and those associated with mentalizing and social judgments. This finding suggests that strong emotional ties to an other (infant or partner) not only inhibit negative feelings, but also impede the functioning of neural networks that might assist in generating social judgements about the attachment figure. These ideas are extremely important and deserve consideration in some detail.

The function of networks deactivated by the attachment system

Although maternal and romantic love clearly serve different functions, they share a number of subjective and objective qualities, such as preoccupation, deep concern, and high level of commitment. Underpinning this may be a common set of brain mechanisms that are activated when attachment feelings are powerfully triggered, but also deactivation of a characteristic set of other neural functions. Bartels and Zeki (2004) suggest grouping these reciprocally active areas into two functional regions. The first (we refer to it as system A) includes the middle prefrontal, inferior parietal, and middle temporal cortices mainly in the right hemisphere, as well as the posterior cingulate cortex. These areas are specialized for attention and long-term memory (Cabeza & Nyberg, 2000) and have variable involvement in both positive (Maddock, 1999) and negative (Mayberg et al., 1999) emotions. Their role in both cognition and emotion suggests that these areas may be specifically responsible for integrating emotion and cognition (e.g., emotional encoding of episodic memories; Maddock, 1999). In addition, studies of individuals who have lesions in these areas suggest a role in judgements involving negative emotions (Adolphs, Damasio, Tranel, Cooper, & Damasio, 2000). It is possible that, as projections from the affect-orientated limbic/paralimbic regions modulate the activity of these areas, they could subserve the ways mood can inhibit or enhance cognitive processing (Mayberg et al., 1999). Further, these areas may play a role in recalling emotion-related material and generating emotion-related imagery (Maddock, 1999) that may be relevant in relation to understanding the typology of attachment.

The second set of areas deactivated by the activation of the attachment system includes the temporal poles, parietotemporal junction, amygdala, and mesial prefrontal cortex (we call this set of areas system B). Activation of these areas is consistently linked to negative affect, judgements of social trustworthiness, moral judgements, "theory of mind" tasks, and attention to one's own emotions, and, in particular, they constitute the primary neural network underlying our ability to identify mental states (both thoughts and feelings) in other people (Frith & Frith, 2003; Gallagher & Frith, 2003). Mentalization pertains not just to states of mind in others, but also reflecting on one's own emotional and belief states and, consequently, such tasks appear to be associated with activation in the same neural system (Gusnard, Akbudak, Shulman, & Raichle, 2001). Making judgements that involve mental states has been shown to be associated with activation of the same system. Thus, intuitive judgements of moral appropriateness (rather than moral reasoning) are linked (Greene & Haidt, 2002), as is assessment of social trustworthiness based on facial expression (Winston, Strange, O'Doherty, & Dolan, 2002).

If confirmed by further studies, the pattern of activation of these three systems (the attachment system, system A, and system B) has important implications for our understanding of the nature of individual differences in attachment, the relationship of attachment, and mentalization and consequently our understanding of dysfunctions associated with BPD and the mechanisms underpinning its psychological treatment. The activation of the attachment system, mediated by dopaminergic structures of the reward system in the presence of oxytocin and vasopressin, inhibits neural systems that underpin the generation of negative affect (system A). This result is to be expected because a key function of the attachment system is to moderate negative affects in the infant and, presumably, later in development (Sroufe, 1996). The overwhelming negative affect associated with the loss of attachment figures, the need for attachment figures at times of sadness, and the hedonic effect of "finding love" are obvious common observations in line with these findings. Not only is the loss of attachment likely to be aversive because of the loss of "reward" (addiction), but also the previous inhibition of systems associated with the generation of negative affect is removed.

Equally consistent with expectations is the suppression of social and moral judgements (system B) associated with the activation of the attachment system. Judgements of social trustworthiness and morality serve to distance us from others but become less relevant to, and may indeed interfere with, our relationships with those to whom we are strongly attached (Belsky, 1999).

Some implications of the reciprocal activation
of mentalization and attachment

The apparently reciprocal relationship of mentalization and attachment is puzzling as, at first sight, it appears to contradict some of the assumptions concerning the facilitative relationship between the two systems outlined earlier (*viz.*, the assumption that mentalization and attachment are positively correlated). Further scrutiny suggests a more complex relationship. First, the neural association between attachment and mentalization confirms the link we have identified between the two systems at a behavioural level (Fonagy, Gergely, Jurist, & Target, 2002). Second, we have demonstrated the

way the parent's capacity to mentalize in the context of an attachment relationship facilitates the development of secure attachment
in the infant (Fonagy, Steele, Moran, Steele, & Higgitt, 1991). It is
possible, taking a sociobiological perspective, that the parent's capacity to mentalize the infant or child serves to reduce the child's experienced need to monitor the parent for trustworthiness. The
relaxation of the interpersonal barrier serves to facilitate the emergence of the attachment bond. Third, we have seen that mentalization emerges precociously in children who were securely attached in
infancy (e.g., Fonagy, Steele, Steele, & Holder, 1997). At first, this
finding may seem inconsistent with the inverse relationship
between attachment and mentalization at brain level; however, if we
consider the association developmentally, it is to be expected that, in
individuals whose attachment is secure, there are likely to be fewer
calls over time for the activation of the attachment system, and that
in turn accounts for the precocious development of mentalization.

Fourth, we have consistently suggested that the capacity for
mentalization in the context of attachment was in some respects
independent of the capacity to mentalize about interpersonal experiences independently of the attachment context (Fonagy, Gergely,
Jurist, & Target, 2002). We have found that our specific measure of
mentalization in the attachment context, reflective function (Fonagy, Target, Steele, & Steele, 1998), is predictive of behavioural
outcomes not correlated with other measures of mentalization. For
example, in a quasi-longitudinal study based on interviews and
chart reviews with young adults, some of whom had suffered
trauma, we found that the impact of trauma on mentalization in
attachment contexts mediated outcome measured as the quality of
adult romantic relationships, but mentalization measured independently of the attachment context using the Reading the Mind in the
Eyes test did not (Fonagy, Stein, Allen, & Fultz, 2003). It seems that
measuring mentalization in the context of attachment measures a
unique aspect of social behaviour.

*Mentalization in the context of attachment and
the classification of attachment types*

Although, from an evolutionary perspective, mentalization may be
generally less relevant in an attachment context than in other social

contexts, nevertheless, it is quite likely that the ability to mentalize in the context of attachment relationships points to a highly desirable capacity. Individuals who are able to mentalize while thinking about romantic partners or infants are likely to manage these relationships better and might, for example, have less turbulent interpersonal relationships, or perhaps be particularly effective at times of inevitable conflict and argument. This could be why secure attachment is marked by a relatively good capacity to mentalize and generate coherent narratives of even turbulent interpersonal episodes (Main, 2000). The simple empirical prediction that follows from these speculations is that individuals who are able to retain a relatively high activation of the temporal lobes, the parietotemporal junction together with the mesial prefrontal cortex (system B), in the presence of the activation of the dopaminergic mesolimbic pathways (attachment and reward system), are those most likely to be classified as secure in their attachment.

A new understanding of the deficit in mentalization in BPD

We have arrived at a new understanding of the deficit of mentalization entailed in borderline personality disorder. We have observed that mentalization in individuals who have BPD frequently represented a challenge described (inappropriately) in the psychoanalytic literature as a failure of symbolization or concreteness of thinking (e.g., Grotstein, 1983). Yet, mentalization in general does not appear to be a problem for most individuals who have BPD; it is only in the context of intimate relationships that the patient's capacity to depict mental states in others accurately appears to falter (Fonagy, Gergely, Jurist, & Target, 2002).

One simple model that may account for this somewhat paradoxical observation is that the attachment system is "hypersensitive", triggered too readily, and consequently the reciprocally deactivated systems are often inefficient (relatively deactivated) in their functioning. Two of the core symptoms of BPD, frantic efforts to avoid real or imagined abandonment and the characteristic pattern of unstable and intense interpersonal relationships characterized by alternating between extremes of idealization and devaluation, are perhaps directly linked to such hyperactivity or hypersensitivity (Gunderson, 2001). A number of frequently noted observations made about individuals who have BPD are consistent with this simple assumption.

1. Relationships of individuals who have BPD have a rapidly escalating tempo moving from acquaintance to great intimacy far faster than one might expect.
2. Hyperactivity of the attachment system removes the system responsible for maintaining a normal emotional barrier between self and others and generates an impression of entangled and preoccupied relationships (Agrawal, Gunderson, Holmes, & Lyons-Ruth, 2004) and frequently, somewhat unwisely, removes the need to assess the social validity of the social partner.
3 The excessively positive character of the initial phase relationships that individuals who have BPD form (often labelled idealization) might reflect the suppression of negative relationship-specific affects and the inability to integrate emotion and cognition.
4. Affective instability, particularly the characteristic intense brief episodes of dysphoria, might be the result of some form of rebound phenomena related to the hypersensitive or hyperactive attachment system. Such rebound effects might also account for outbursts of violent anger and interpersonal suspiciousness (paranoia), which might reflect overactivity in system B (Pickup & Frith, 2001).
5. The reduction of the influence of affectively laden episodic memory might relate to the chronic feelings of emptiness often encountered by individuals who have this diagnosis.

Of central concern to our theoretical and clinical propositions is the mentalization deficit we have reported in these patients (Fonagy et al., 1996). While standing by our description of the mental processes that emerge as characteristic of the intentional stance of the individual who has BPD, we would now like to specify the cause of this deficit. Previously, we have argued that the deficit was a self-induced one—a defensive reaction in vulnerable individuals when confronted with hostile states of mind in the context of interpersonal trauma. Although many of the extant data still appear to us to fit with this model (e.g., the association of early neglect with

BPD, the undermining of the development of symbolization in the families of maltreated youngsters, the high prevalence of attachment trauma, the high prevalence of individuals who show no BPD symptoms after trauma), it seems highly likely that mentalization deficit can be secondary to the abnormal functioning of the attachment system (i.e., its hyperactivity). The latter, of course, is likely to be the consequence of developmentally early dysfunctions of the attachment system in combination with later traumatic experiences in an attachment context. We speculate that deficits of mentalization might sometimes occur because the capacity to mentalize is taken offline by the activation of the attachment system. Of course, this is not an "all or nothing affair." We assume that, in these individuals, who are insecurely attached and therefore would not be able to maintain mentalization normally in any case in the context of attachment relationships, the hyperresponsiveness of the attachment system, perhaps related to traumatic or other early experiences or genetic predisposition, has an unusually negative impact upon mentalizing with the expected effects already described. It remains probable that activating the capacity to mentalize in the context of attachment relationships generates substantial anxiety for traumatized individuals, which in turn increases the activation of the attachment system in even those who have an avoidant-dismissing pattern of attachment. Of course, here we have a potentially extremely vicious cycle of heightened attachment, increasingly decoupled mentalization, and increased vulnerability to further interpersonal trauma. A number of testable hypotheses follow from this model. Predictions from this model include the following.

1. Mentalization dysfunctions should be observable only when the attachment system is active.
2. Mentalization dysfunction should be associated with negative affect.
3. Problems of accurate social and moral judgments should correlate with mentalization capacity.
4. The degree of disorganization of attachment relationships should correlate with the likelihood of mentalization problems.
5. There are likely to be deficits associated with the retrieval of emotion-laden memories when the attachment system is active.

6.   Ambiguous stimuli (e.g., polysemous words with attachment and non-attachment meanings) are more likely to trigger the attachment system of BPD individuals.

Implications for therapy and the mechanisms of change

How can this model of the nature of deficit in BPD serve to focus our work with BPD patients, or, rather, how do we understand the changes we observe given the current focus of our work, which is to assist in the recovery of the capacity to think accurately about thoughts or feelings? There is an important proviso to this aim. MBT, in a range of contexts, attempts to enhance mentalization, but always in the context of an attachment relationship. Both in individual and in group therapy, the therapist, through a range of largely unconscious techniques, activates the attachment system. This activation occurs through (1) the discussion of current attachment relationships, (2) the discussion of past attachment relationships, (3) the therapist's encouragement and regulation of the patient's attachment bond to him or her through the creation of an environment that assists with the patient's regulation of affect, (4) the therapist's attempt to engender attachment bonds between members of the group in the context of group therapy. At the same time, paradoxically, the therapist attempts to enhance mentalization not just in the techniques defined in the therapy manual, but, perhaps more importantly and generically, simply by his or her interest in the mental world of the patient. This interest creates what we now understand as a somewhat paradoxical situation in terms of brain activity in so far as psychological therapy simultaneously activates what may be two mutually inhibitory sets of systems. There are two other ways in which this somewhat paradoxical pattern of activation is maintained: (1) the titrated activation of negative emotions as the therapist encourages the confrontation of adverse or traumatic experiences, and (2) the encouragement to retrieve affect-laden episodic memories. In these ways, the individual who has BPD is encouraged to counteract the normal pattern of attachment-related deactivation of mentalizing of negative emotions and social and moral judgements.

We can see that, overall, MBT encourages the patient not to relinquish mentalization at the slightest suggestion of attachment-related brain activation. This is likely to have an impact on the attachment system as well, because we have seen that mentalization strengthens the development of secure patterns of attachment. In other words, at the same time as strengthening mentalization, we speculate that MBT moves the pattern of arousal within these systems closer to that characteristic of a secure attachment. Evidently, to achieve this aim the therapist must be careful to balance the intensity of attachment relationships and the complexity of mentalization required of the patient. The technical recommendation in MBT is to focus the patient's mentalization on relationships that have relatively low levels of involvement and only gradually to focus the patient's thinking on relationships closer to the patient's core self. Similarly, the tasks of mentalization vary in demand characteristics, with clarification at the most superficial end and exploring of repudiated intense emotions in relation to the attachment figure at the more complex end. The therapist's aim is to reduce the likelihood of an anxious catastrophic response to the introduction of the need to think about the states of mind of attachment figures.

Thus, using this model may help us to differentiate it from alternative therapeutic packages. Although such distinctions are never more than caricatures, they do point to important differences in technique between therapeutic approaches that are probably broadly equivalent in terms of achieving substantial therapeutic change. Thus, aspects of DBT clearly also focus on the enhancing of mentalization, such as the encouragement of mindfulness. However, this process rarely occurs in the context of requiring individuals to conceptualize mental states in the context of attachment relationships. By contrast, supportive psychotherapy is less specifically focused on mental states, but probably attempts to reduce the hypersensitivity of the attachment system of an individual who suffered severe attachment trauma. Transference-focused psychotherapy is perhaps closest to MBT in its orientation to mental states in attachment contexts; the difference is a far more limited emphasis on the titration of interventions. The observations (Levy et al., 2006) are consistent with the propositions here: attachment-related mentalization (reflective function) improves only in transference focused psychotherapy (TFP) and not in DBT or supportive psychotherapy.

Implications for the general process of change in therapy

The therapeutic process we have described in relation to MBT with BPD is probably not specific to either this approach or this patient group. A strong case can be made that all forms of psychotherapy take some advantage of the simultaneous activation of these normally mutually inhibitory systems. It is possible that psychotherapy in general is effective because it arouses the attachment system at the same time it applies interpersonal demands (psychotherapy technique), which require the patient to mentalize, to confront and experience negative affect, and to confront and review issues of morality (superego). Why might this be helpful? We speculate that thinking about feelings, thoughts, and beliefs in the context of attachment is helpful because in this "paradoxical" brain state there may be more access to modifying preset ways of conceptualizing the contents of one's own and other's minds, as well as issues of morality and social judgement. Activating the attachment system harnesses brain biological processes partially to remove the dominance of constraints on the present from the past (long-term memory) and creates the possibility of rethinking, reconfiguring intersubjective relationship networks. The specific advantage of MBT in this process might be its focus on the simultaneous activation of the attachment system and encouragement of development of psychological processes that are normally inhibited as a result. To this extent, MBT represents a confluence of biology and psychology and goes some way towards meeting Kazdin's edict that an understanding of the processes underpinning psychopathology should inform treatment innovation.

Note

1. A more fully referenced version of this chapter is available from the authors on request.

References

Adolphs, R. (2003). Cognitive neuroscience of human social behaviour. *Nature Reviews*, 4: 165–178.

Adolphs, R., Damasio, H., Tranel, D., Cooper, G., & Damasio, A. R. (2000). A role for somatosensory cortices in the visual recognition of emotion as revealed by three-dimensional lesion mapping. *Journal of Neuroscience, 20*(7): 2683–2690.

Agrawal, H. R., Gunderson, J., Holmes, B. M., & Lyons-Ruth, K. (2004). Attachment studies with borderline patients: a review. *Harvard Review of Psychiatry, 12*(2): 94–104.

Arnsten, A. F. T. (1998). The biology of being frazzled. *Science, 280*: 1711–1712.

Arntz, A., & Veen, G. (2001). Evaluations of others by borderline patients. *Journal of Nervous and Mental Disease, 189*(8): 513–521.

Barone, L. (2003). Developmental protective and risk factors in borderline personality disorder: a study using the Adult Attachment Interview. *Attachment and Human Development, 5*(1): 64–77.

Bartels, A., & Zeki, S. (2000). The neural basis of romantic love. *Neuroreport, 11*(17): 3829–3834.

Bartels, A., & Zeki, S. (2004). The neural correlates of maternal and romantic love. *Neuroimage, 21*(3): 1155–1166.

Bateman, A. W., & Fonagy, P. (1999). The effectiveness of partial hospitalization in the treatment of borderline personality disorder—a randomised controlled trial. *American Journal of Psychiatry, 156*, 1563–1569.

Bateman, A. W., & Fonagy, P. (2001). Treatment of borderline personality disorder with psychoanalytically oriented partial hospitalization: an 18-month follow-up. *American Journal of Psychiatry, 158*(1): 36–42.

Bateman, A. W., & Fonagy, P. (2003). Health service utilization costs for borderline personality disorder patients treated with psychoanalytically oriented partial hospitalization versus general psychiatric care. *American Journal of Psychiatry, 160*(1): 169–171.

Bateman, A. W., & Fonagy, P. (2004). *Psychotherapy for Borderline Personality Disorder: Mentalization Based Treatment.* Oxford: Oxford University Press.

Battle, C. L., Shea, M. T., Johnson, D. M., Yen, S., Zlotnick, C., Zanarini, M. C., Sanislow, C. A., Skodol, A. E., Gunderson, J. G., Grilo, C. M., McGlashan, T. H., & Morey, L. C. (2004). Childhood maltreatment associated with adult personality disorders: findings from the Collaborative Longitudinal Personality Disorders Study. *Journal of Personality Disorders, 18*(2): 193–211.

Bazanis, E., Rogers, R. D., Dowson, J. H., Taylor, P., Meux, C., Staley, C., Nevinson-Andrews, D., Taylor, C., Robbins, T. W., & Sahakian, B. J. (2002). Neurocognitive deficits in decision-making and planning of patients with DSM-III-R borderline personality disorder. *Psychological Medicine, 32*(8): 1395–1405.

Belsky, J. (1999). Modern evolutionary theory and patterns of attachment. In: J. Cassidy & P.R. Shaver (Eds.), *Handbook of Attachment: Theory, Research and Clinical Applications* (pp. 141–161). New York: Guilford Press.

Bleiberg, E., Fonagy, P., & Target, M. (1997). Child psychoanalysis: critical overview and a proposed reconsideration. *Psychiatric Clinics of North America, 6*: 1–38.

Cabeza, R., & Nyberg, L. (2000). Neural bases of learning and memory: functional neuroimaging evidence. *Current Opinion in Neurology, 13*(4): 415–421.

Cardinal, R. N., Pennicott, D. R., Sugathapala, C. L., Robbins, T. W., & Everitt, B. J. (2001). Impulsive choice induced in rats by lesions of the nucleus accumbens core. *Science, 292*(5526): 2499–2501.

Carpendale, J. I. M., & Lewis, C. (2004). Constructing an understanding of mind: the development of children's social understanding within social interaction. *Behavioral and Brain Sciences, 27*: 79–151.

Crandell, L. E., Patrick, M. P. H., & Hobson, R. P. (2003). "Still-face" interactions between mothers with borderline personality disorder and their 2-month-old infants. *British Journal of Psychiatry, 183*, 239–247.

Critchley, H., Daly, E., Phillips, M., Brammer, M., Bullmore, E., Williams, S., Van Amelsvoort, T., Robertson, D., David, A., & Murphy, D. (2000). Explicit and implicit neural mechanisms for processing of social information from facial expressions: a functional magnetic resonance imaging study. *Human Brain Mapping, 9*(2): 93–105.

Crittenden, P. M. (1997). Toward an integrative theory of trauma: a dynamic-maturation approach. In: D. Cicchetti & S. L. Toth (Eds.), *Rochester Symposium on Developmental Psychopathology: Developmental Perspectives on Trauma* (Volume 8) (pp. 33–84). Rochester, NY: University of Rochester Press.

Daruna, J. H., & Barnes, P. A. (1993). A neurodevelopmental view of impulsivity. In: W. G. McCann, J. L. Johnson, & M. B. Shire (Eds.), *The Impulsive Client: Theory, Research and Treatment* (pp. 76–89). Washington, DC: American Psychological Association.

De Bellis, M. D., Keshavan, M. S., Spencer, S., & Hall, J. (2000). *N*-acetyl-aspartate concentration in the anterior cingulate of maltreated children and adolescents with PTSD. *American Journal of Psychiatry, 157*: 1175–1177.

Dougherty, D. M., Bjork, J. M., Huckabee, H. C., Moeller, F. G., & Swann, A. C. (1999). Laboratory measures of aggression and impulsivity in women with borderline personality disorder. *Psychiatry Research, 85*(3): 315–326.

Everitt, B. J., & Wolf, M. E. (2002). Psychomotor stimulant addiction: a neural systems perspective. *Journal of Neuroscience, 22*(9): 3312–3320.

Flavell, J. H., & Miller, P. H. (1998). Social cognition. In: W. Damon, D. Kuhn, & R. S. Siegler (Eds.), *Handbook of Child Psychology* (5th edn) (pp. 851–898). New York: Wiley.

Fonagy, P. (1989). On tolerating mental states: theory of mind in borderline patients. *Bulletin of the Anna Freud Centre, 12*: 91–115.

Fonagy, P. (1991). Thinking about thinking: some clinical and theoretical considerations in the treatment of a borderline patient. *International Journal of Psychoanalysis, 72*: 1–18.

Fonagy, P., Gergely, G., Jurist, E., & Target, M. (2002). *Affect Regulation, Mentalization and The Development of The Self.* New York: Other Press.

Fonagy, P., Leigh, T., Steele, M., Steele, H., Kennedy, R., Mattoon, G., Target, M., & Gerber, A. (1996). The relation of attachment status, psychiatric classification, and response to psychotherapy. *Journal of Consulting and Clinical Psychology, 64*: 22–31.

Fonagy, P., Steele, H., Moran, G., Steele, M., & Higgitt, A. (1991). The capacity for understanding mental states: the reflective self in parent and child and its significance for security of attachment. *Infant Mental Health Journal, 13*, 200–217.

Fonagy, P., Steele, H., Steele, M., & Holder, J. (1997). Attachment and theory of mind: overlapping constructs? *Association for Child Psychology and Psychiatry Occasional Papers, 14*: 31–40.

Fonagy, P., Stein, H., Allen, J., & Fultz, J. (2003). The relationship of mentalization and childhood and adolescent adversity to adult functioning. Paper presented at the Biennial Meeting of the Society for Research in Child Development, Tampa, FL.

Fonagy, P., Target, M., & Gergely, G. (2000). Attachment and borderline personality disorder: a theory and some evidence. *Psychiatric Clinics of North America, 23*, 103–122.

Fonagy, P., Target, M., Steele, H., & Steele, M. (1998). *Reflective-Functioning Manual, Version 5.0, for Application to Adult Attachment Interviews*. London: University College London.

Freud, A. (1936). *The Ego and The Mechanisms of Defence*. New York: International Universities Press, 1946.

Frith, U., & Frith, C. D. (2003). Development and neurophysiology of mentalizing. *Philosophical Transactions of the Royal Society of London B, Biological Sciences, 358*: 459–473.

Gallagher, H. L., & Frith, C. D. (2003). Functional imaging of "theory of mind". *Trends in Cognitive Science, 7*(2): 77–83.

Gallagher, H. L., Happe, F., Brunswick, N., Fletcher, P. C., Frith, U., & Frith, C. D. (2000). Reading the mind in cartoons and stories: an fMRI study of "theory of mind" in verbal and nonverbal tasks. *Neuropsychologia, 38*(1): 11–21.

Gingrich, B., Liu, Y., Cascio, C., Wang, Z., & Insel, T. R. (2000). Dopamine D2 receptors in the nucleus accumbens are important for social attachment in female prairie voles (*Microtus ochrogaster*). *Behavioral Neuroscience, 114*(1): 173–183.

Gopnik, A. (1993). How we know our minds: the illusion of first-person knowledge of intentionality. *Behavioral and Brain Sciences, 16*: 1–14, 29–113.

Greene, J., & Haidt, J. (2002). How (and where) does moral judgment work? *Trends in Cognitive Science, 6*(12): 517–523.

Grotstein, J. (1983). A proposed revision of the psychoanalytic concept of primitive mental states: Part 2. The borderline syndrome-Section 1. Disorders of autistic safety and symbiotic relatedness. *Contemporary Psychoanalysis, 19*: 570–604.

Gunderson, J. G. (1996). The borderline patient's intolerance of aloneness: insecure attachments and therapist availability. *American Journal of Psychiatry, 153*(6): 752–758.

Gunderson, J. G. (2001). *Borderline Personality Disorder: A Clinical Guide*. Washington, DC: American Psychiatric Association.

Gunderson, J. G., Bender, D., Sanislow, C., Yen, S., Rettew, J. B., Dolan-Sewell, R., Dyck, I., Morey, L. C., McGlashan, T. H., Shea, M. T., & Skodol, A. E. (2003). Plausibility and possible determinants of sudden "remissions" in borderline patients. *Psychiatry, 66*(2): 111–119.

Gusnard, D. A., Akbudak, E., Shulman, G. L., & Raichle, M. E. (2001). Medial prefrontal cortex and self-referential mental activity: relation to a default mode of brain function. *Proceedings of the National Academy of Sciences, 98*(7): 4259–4264.

Holmes, J. (2003). Borderline personality disorder and the search for meaning: an attachment perspective. *Australian and New Zealand Journal of Psychiatry*, 37(5): 524–531.

Insel, T. R. (2003). Is social attachment an addictive disorder? *Physiology & Behavior*, 79(3): 351–357.

Insel, T. R., & Young, L. J. (2000). Neuropeptides and the evolution of social behavior. *Current Opinion in Neurobiology*, 10(6): 784–789.

Kawabata, H., & Zeki, S. (2004). Neural correlates of beauty. *Journal of Neurophysiology*, 91(4): 1699–1705.

Kazdin, A. E. (2004). Psychotherapy for children and adolescents. In: M. Lambert (Ed.), *Bergin and Garfield's Handbook of Psychotherapy and Behavior Change* (5th edn) (pp. 543–589). New York: Wiley.

Koob, G. F., & Le Moal, M. (1997). Drug abuse: hedonic homeostatic dysregulation. *Science*, 278(5335): 52–58.

Lane, R. D. (2000). Neural correlates of conscious emotional experience. In: R. D. Lane & L. Nadel (Eds.), *Cognitive Neuroscience of Emotion* (pp. 345–370). New York: Oxford University Press.

Lee, A., Li, M., Watchus, J., & Fleming, A. S. (1999). Neuroanatomical basis of maternal memory in postpartum rats: selective role for the nucleus accumbens. *Behavioral Neuroscience*, 113(3): 523–538.

Leihener, F., Wagner, A., Haaf, B., Schmidt, C., Lieb, K., Stieglitz, R., & Bohus, M. (2003). Subtype differentiation of patients with borderline personality disorder using a circumplex model of interpersonal behavior. *Journal of Nervous and Mental Disease*, 191(4): 248–254.

Levy, K. N., Clarkin, J. F., Yeomans, F. E., Scott, L. N., Wasserman, R. H., & Kernberg, O. F. (2006). The mechanisms of change in the treatment of borderline personality disorder with transference focused psychotherapy. *Journal of Clinical Psychology*, 62(4): 481–501.

Lim, M. M., & Young, L. J. (2004). Vasopressin-dependent neural circuits underlying pair bond formation in the monogamous prairie vole. *Neuroscience*, 125(1): 35–45.

Lim, M. M., Murphy, A. Z., & Young, L. J. (2004). Ventral striatopallidal oxytocin and vasopressin V1a receptors in the monogamous prairie vole (Microtus ochrogaster). *Journal of Comparative Neurology*, 468(4): 555–570.

Lim, M. M., Wang, Z., Olazabal, D. E., Ren, X., Terwilliger, E. F., & Young, L. J. (2004). Enhanced partner preference in a promiscuous species by manipulating the expression of a single gene. *Nature*, 429(6993): 754–757.

Linehan, M. M., Dimeff, L. A., Reynolds, S. K., Comtois, K. A., Welch, S. S., Heagerty, P., & Kivlahan, D. R. (2002). Dialectical behavior therapy versus comprehensive validation therapy plus 12-step for the treatment of opioid dependent women meeting criteria for borderline personality disorder. *Drug and Alcohol Dependence*, 67(1): 13–26.

Liotti, G. (2002). The inner schema of borderline states and its correction during psychotherapy: a cognitive–evolutionary approach. *Journal of Cognitive Psychotherapy*, 16, 349–366.

Lyons-Ruth, K., & Jacobovitz, D. (1999). Attachment disorganization: unresolved loss, relational violence and lapses in behavioral and attentional strategies. In: J. Cassidy & P. R. Shaver (Eds.), *Handbook of Attachment Theory and Research* (pp. 520–554). New York: Guilford.

MacLean, P. (1990). *The Triune Brain in Evolution: Role in Paleocerebral Functions*. New York: Plenum Press.

Maddock, R. J. (1999). The retrosplenial cortex and emotion: new insights from functional neuroimaging of the human brain. *Trends in Neuroscience*, 22(7): 310–316.

Main, M. (2000). The organized categories of infant, child and adult attachment: flexible vs. inflexible attention under attachment-related stress. *Journal of the American Psychoanalytic Association*, 48(4): 1055–1096.

Mayberg, H. S., Liotti, M., Brannan, S. K., McGinnis, S., Mahurin, R. K., Jerabek, P. A., Silva, J. A., Tekell, J. L., Martin, C. C., Lancaster, J. L., & Fox, P. T. (1999). Reciprocal limbic-cortical function and negative mood: converging PET findings in depression and normal sadness. *American Journal of Psychiatry*, 156(5): 675–682.

Meins, E., Fernyhough, C., Russel, J., & Clark-Carter, D. (1998). Security of attachment as a predictor of symbolic and mentalising abilities: a longitudinal study. *Social Development*, 7: 1–24.

Nitschke, J. B., Nelson, E. E., Rusch, B. D., Fox, A. S., Oakes, T. R., & Davidson, R. J. (2004). Orbitofrontal cortex tracks positive mood in mothers viewing pictures of their newborn infants. *Neuroimage*, 21(2): 583–592.

Panksepp, J. (1998). *Affective Neuroscience: The Foundations of Human and Animal Emotions*. Oxford: Oxford University Press.

Patrick, M., Hobson, R. P., Castle, D., Howard, R., & Maughan, B. (1994). Personality disorder and the mental representation of early social experience. *Developmental Psychopathology*, 6, 375–388.

Pickup, G. J., & Frith, C. D. (2001). Theory of mind impairments in schizophrenia: symptomatology, severity and specificity. *Psychological Medicine*, 31(2): 207-220.

Posner, M. I., Rothbart, M. K., Vizueta, N., Levy, K. N., Evans, D. E., Thomas, K. M., & Clarkin, J. F. (2002). Attentional mechanisms of borderline personality disorder. *Proceedings of the National Academy of Sciences, 99*(25): 16366–16370.

Rogers, R. D., Everitt, B. J., Baldacchino, A., Blackshaw, A. J., Swainson, R., Wynne, K., Baker, N. B., Hunter, J., Carthy, T., Booker, E., London, M., Deakin, J. F., Sahakian, B. J., & Robbins, T. W. (1999). Dissociable deficits in the decision-making cognition of chronic amphetamine abusers, opiate abusers, patients with focal damage to prefrontal cortex, and tryptophan-depleted normal volunteers: evidence for monoaminergic mechanisms. *Neuropsychopharmacology, 20*(4): 322–339.

Roth, A., & Fonagy, P. (2005). *What Works For Whom? A Critical Review of Psychotherapy Research* (2nd edn). New York: Guilford Press.

Sayar, K., Ebrinc, S., & Ak, I. (2001). Alexithymia in patients with anti-social personality disorder in a military hospital setting. *Israel Journal of Psychiatry and Related Science, 38*(2): 81–87.

Silk, K. R. (2000). Borderline personality disorder: overview of biologic factors. *Psychiatric Clinics of North America, 23*(1): 61–75.

Skodol, A. E., Gunderson, J. G., McGlashan, T. H., Dyck, I. R., Stout, R. L., Bender, D. S., Grilo, C. M., Shea, M. T., Zanarini, M. C., Morey, L. C., Sanislow, C. A., & Oldham, J. M. (2002a). Functional impairment in patients with schizotypal, borderline, avoidant, or obsessive-compulsive personality disorder. *American Journal of Psychiatry, 159*(2): 276–283.

Skodol, A. E., Gunderson, J. G., Pfohl, B., Widiger, T. A., Livesley, W. J., & Siever, L. J. (2002b). The borderline diagnosis: 1. Psychopathology, comorbidity and personality and personality strucutre. *Biological Psychiatry, 51*(12): 936–950.

Skodol, A. E., Siever, L. J., Livesley, W. J., Gunderson, J. G., Pfohl, B., & Widiger, T. A. (2002c). The borderline diagnosis: 2. Biology, genetics, and clinical course. *Biological Psychiatry, 51*(12): 951–963.

Sroufe, L. A. (1996). *Emotional Development: The Organization of Emotional Life in The Early Years.* New York: Cambridge University Press.

Stack, E. C., Balakrishnan, R., Numan, M. J., & Numan, M. (2002). A functional neuroanatomical investigation of the role of the medial preoptic area in neural circuits regulating maternal behavior. *Behavioural and Brain Research, 131*(1–2): 17–36.

Strathearn, L., & McClure, S. M. (2002). A functional MRI study of maternal responses of infant facial cues. Paper presented at the

Annual Scientific Meeting of the Society for Neuroscience. Abstract Viewer/Itinerary Planner, Program No. 517.5. Online. Washington, DC.

Torgersen, S., Lygren, S., Oien, P. A., Skre, I., Onstad, S., Edvardsen, J., Tambs, K., & Kringlen, E. (2000). A twin study of personality disorders. *Comprehensive Psychiatry*, 41(6): 416–425.

Trull, T. J. (2001). Structural relations between borderline personality disorder features and putative etiological correlates. *Journal of Abnormal Psychology*, 110(3): 471–481.

Vernotica, E. M., Rosenblatt, J. S., & Morrell, J. I. (1999). Microinfusion of cocaine into the medial preoptic area or nucleus accumbens transiently impairs maternal behavior in the rat. *Behavioral Neuroscience*, 113(2): 377–390.

Wang, Z., Yu, G., Cascio, C., Liu, Y., Gingrich, B., & Insel, T. R. (1999). Dopamine D2 receptor-mediated regulation of partner preferences in female prairie voles (*Microtus ochrogaster*): a mechanism for pair bonding? *Behavioral Neuroscience*, 113(3): 602–611.

Winnicott, D. W. (1956). Mirror role of mother and family in child development. In: D. W. Winnicott (Ed.), *Playing and Reality* (pp. 111–118). London: Tavistock.

Winston, J. S., Strange, B. A., O'Doherty, J., & Dolan, R. J. (2002). Automatic and intentional brain responses during evaluation of trustworthiness of faces. *Nature Neuroscience*, 5(3): 277–283.

Young, L. J., Lim, M. M., Gingrich, B., & Insel, T. R. (2001). Cellular mechanisms of social attachment. *Hormones and Behavior*, 40(2): 133–138.

Zanarini, M. C., Frankenburg, F. R., Hennen, J., & Silk, K. R. (2003). The longitudinal course of borderline psychopathology: 6-year prospective follow-up of the phenomenology of borderline personality disorder. *American Journal of Psychiatry*, 160(2): 274–283.

CHAPTER FOUR

Discussion of "Mechanisms of change in mentalization-based treatment of borderline personality disorder" by Peter Fonagy and Anthony Bateman

Robin Anderson

M any years ago, when I began my psychiatry training at the Maudsley Hospital, my first placement was under Dr Ted Hare, who said, in a reasonably even-handed way, that psychiatrists tended either to develop a special interest in research or in psychotherapy, and it was not long after that that I decided that my future lay in psychotherapy. Perhaps this was an unfortunate classification which I seemed to have rather too quickly internalized. However, in one sense I think he was drawing attention to those of us who, despite medical training (the field for scientists who cannot do maths!), had an interest in an understanding of humanity and the human condition of a more philosophical literary kind. When I first came across Henri Rey at the Maudsley, it was not so much his complex classification of psychosis that first grabbed me; it was the way he could succinctly describe the essence of a patient's dilemma in a simple and compassionate way which both moved and greatly impressed me. I had a similar emotional experience and depth that I get from a work of literature, or, say, from watching a Beckett play. How did he get there from the same data that I had just heard and yet had not even left first base? So, that was what I went looking for, and I found it, or at least the path to it, through psychoanalysis: my own and later, that of my patients.

The satisfaction of being able to have a shared experience of profound understanding arrived at after hard painful work by patient and analyst is deeply satisfying. This satisfying experience carried with it a deep sense of conviction to patient and analyst/ therapist, and I found that it would often lead to permanent change, usually slowly, but sometimes surprisingly quickly. Some- times, in the context of very disturbed suicidal patients, one had the conviction that one had saved their lives, and in others that one had opened up possibilities for them that it was hard to believe could have happened in any other way. Of course, not all patients could be helped, and I found that we were not that good at deciding in advance who might benefit most. It did not seem to be related just to the severity. As Peter Fonagy and Anthony Bateman have shown, some borderline patients could change dramatically. In considering psychotherapy as a treatment, some take the view that psycho- analysis is an endeavour that is a quite different kind of investiga- tion and, for some, not a treatment at all. This was not Freud's view, and his statement that psychoanalysis is the transformation of neurosis into ordinary human unhappiness, like so many of his aphorisms, condenses so much, but one could say of it that the helping of our patients to be ordinarily unhappy can help them find peace and, paradoxically, even happiness, and this is certainly a worthy treatment outcome. Others, therefore, including myself, and certainly those working in the public sector, do see psychoanalysis as a treatment in the widest sense.

I also came to the view that shedding the more empirical approach has its price, not because psychoanalysis and psychother- apy do not make their own discoveries through rigorous investiga- tion, which I believe have real validity, but because it can isolate itself from its neighbours and, as we have just seen so eloquently presented, some of the neighbours are very close. The mind that we study in our own unique way is situated in a brain. This brain– mind is studied by psychoanalysts, using their own special instru- ment, themselves, which has been modified to be able to process mental phenomena, using conscious and unconscious means, and, therefore, a mind can study a mind in a way that depends on the special communication that is unique to our species. However, its special findings do not answer all the questions that we need to ask.

My first sense that the ignoring of empirical research was not a very good idea came when I was part of the management of the Tavistock Clinic, and we found that even with the most skilled politics we were finding it hard to convince those funding us that we were doing something worthwhile. We knew that we were, but we were moving into a world where funding was getting more controlled and auditors and commissioners were beginning to realize that one of the ways of managing the spiralling costs of the NHS was to "weed out" the ineffective treatments. This takeover of empirical science by cost controllers became the basis of "Evidence based medicine", that wonderful fundamentalist device that has been so unquestionably accepted. I distinctly remember that Peter Fonagy, who had been appointed to develop a national policy on psychotherapy, came to the rescue by saying with conviction, with regard to the paucity of empirical evidence for the effectiveness of psychoanalytic psychotherapy, that lack of evidence did not mean the same as ineffectiveness. None the less, we soon realized that this "psychoanalysis is special and different" category would not last: it was a haven, but not a very safe one, and so, with a gun at our heads, together with others, we began to think about empirical research in psychoanalytic psychotherapy. The Depression Study in the Adult Department at the Tavistock Clinic was led by another psychoanalyst, Professor Phil Richardson, and although I found some of the discussions very uncomfortable, especially issues such as randomization of patients, I did see that even manualized psychoanalytic work, when done by experienced psychotherapists, did seem to pass the test for me of work that had depth and resonance. This could begin to give us the evidence that we need to show that our work is effective. I began to accept that we must not turn our backs on research and that it might do more for us than simply demonstrate effectiveness.

Peter's and Anthony's work, of course, goes much further than finding empirically measurable categories in order to demonstrate effectiveness, and when we think about the enormous difficulty that psychotherapy has had in finding really meaningful measures, here are measures of something that is pretty close to measures of failed containment. Peter and Anthony are able to show that transference focused psychotherapy is much more effective than supportive psychotherapy. Again, we can feel relieved and say, "I told you so", but there are other findings that challenge us. "Interpretations about the past do not help" in working with borderline patients or "the aim is not insight, but the recovery of mentalization". We are giving our patients an experience of our trying to understand their minds, and so they will develop an interest in this, too. I sense from the work that Peter and Anthony gave me to read, though I have not heard much of the actual clinical work, that there are some issues about analytic work of which they do not speak. Is there any place for mental pain in their schema? It is a consistent finding in psychoanalysis that change comes from the ability to begin to bear psychic pain and frustration. Projective identification is a relief to the mental apparatus, and so the taking back of a projection requires the capacity to bear the pain of owning a feeling. Peter and Anthony make links to the paranoid–schizoid position, but we would say that to move to the depressive position means to tolerate the pain of an imperfect world, even a world that the child, in his omnipotent psychic equivalent world, feels he has created. When he accepts a more real view of his psychic world then he feels pain, guilt, and sadness. That is what the analyst has to help him to bear. In other words, mentalizing means facing something against a pressure not to do so, to project, ignore, or switch to more primitive areas of the brain. Not to do this requires an ability to bear something that, if the mother/analyst can do so, allows this function to be internalized. Can this dynamic find a place in this schema?

My limited ability to follow the neurobiological approaches means I can do less than justice to this complex and thorough body of work, but I can say that I think that there is a debate to be had with mainstream psychoanalysis as to what has to be revisited and questioned and, on the other hand, when our own sense of conviction is so strong that it means we must ask Peter and Anthony to go back to their findings to see if they are being too simple. None the less, I believe that a creative dialogue is vital for both sides of this mind–body barrier, and that their work will continue to develop and sometimes help us and sometimes challenge us, and sometimes be challenged by us.

CHAPTER FIVE

Exploring the inner world in a patient suffering from manic-depression

Trudie Rossouw

Introduction

In this chapter, I am hoping to explore the inner world of a patient suffering from bipolar affective disorder (BPAD), here referred to as manic-depressive illness. Psychiatric research strongly suggests the existence of organic pathology in bipolar affective disorder. (McGuffin et al.'s [2003] genetic studies show marked heritability associated with bipolar affective disorder. Farmer, Eley, and McGuffin (2005) recently emphasized that what is inherited is a genetic vulnerability that then requires certain environmental factors to trigger genetic transcription. Haldane and Frangou (2004) used neuroimaging technology to suggest there are permanent structural brain changes associated with the disorder. Savitz, Solms, and Rajkumar (2005) neurocognitive studies illustrated deficits in both the acute and remittance phases. Psychoanalysts such as Fenichel (1945), Jacobson (1971), and Loeb and Loeb (1987) have also argued biological factors to be causative in mania.) This chapter is not entering into an either/or debate; organic *vs.* psychological. It is hoping to explore the psychic life of a patient suffering from an organic disorder. I am also not hoping to make generalized

statements about the inner world of BPAD in general; it is an exploration of the psychic life of one case. The only generalized comment
which would be applicable is the obvious one, in that all patients
suffering from so-called organic conditions or mental illness still
have a psychic world populated by internal objects and object relations, which play a role in how the condition is expressed and,
indeed, are influenced by the condition itself. Even though someone
may be in need of psychiatric intervention and medication, it does
not preclude the fact that the person has a rich inner world, exploration of which would hope to bring meaning and hence containment.

Psychoanalysis offers something unique, for it allows us to
observe and come closer to understanding the intimate subjective
experience (conscious and unconscious) of our patients' minds. A
patient suffering from manic-depressive illness lives a stormy life.
Their internal and external relationships are influenced as the affective tides inherent in the cyclical phases of the condition change.
However, this is also our opportunity; our challenge is to see if
analytic treatment can alter the intensity of the storms and render
them less dangerous.

I once overheard two orthopaedic colleagues having a conversation over lunch, and the one said to the other, "I saw such an interesting hip this morning." It made me think how easy it is to reduce
a person to a condition. What I am aware of in my analytic work
with the case that I am going to present is the complex interplay
between the "mental illness" and the patient, the person. The person, through inheritance and experience, evolves a unique character
structure; this shapes how he/she organizes all aspects of experience, including their internal worlds and the ways they view and
respond to the external world. The analysis of patients with these
conditions, however, opens a window on the way these processes
interact, shape, and form each other, and it is this subtle, intricate
interplay which this report aims, very inadequately, to describe.

Literature review

Melancholia

Abraham was the first psychoanalyst to treat manic-depressive
patients. His understanding of depressed patients was that they

suffered from a paralysis of love because of the overwhelming nature of their sadistic fantasies (1911). Following Freud's description of the developmental stages of libidinal development, he subdivided the oral and the anal stage into two sub-phases; the oral phase, comprising a pre-ambivalent sucking phase, followed by an ambivalent phase, with ambivalence between sucking and biting. The early anal phase is linked to the evacuation and destruction of the object and the later anal phase is linked to retaining and controlling the object. He viewed the fixation points for depression to be at both the ambivalent oral phase and the early anal phase, both phases being dominated by sadistic fantasies. He viewed both mania and depression as arising from repression of the sadistic impulses and the difference in symptomatology as due to a difference in the patient's attitude to the same complex. He also postulated that depression in adults possibly has its roots in infancy, a view that was later expanded by Klein.

In "Mourning and melancholia" (1917e) Freud suggested that both conditions were responses to a loss, the difference being that in melancholia there is a distinctive loss in self-esteem and self-regard expressed as self-reproaches. He said, "In mourning it is the world which has become poor and empty; in melancholia it is the ego itself" (p. 246).

Freud viewed the self-reproaches of the melancholic as accusations against the object. In his view, the object lost is introjected and then identified with. The object gets reinstated in the ego as the ego becomes identified with it. The libido originally attached to the object becomes withdrawn into the ego. This sets up a narcissistic cathexis of the ego. The aggression originally aimed at the disappointing object therefore has been transformed into a conflict between what Freud called then "the critical activity of the ego" (later to be known as the superego) and the ego. The "critical activity of the ego" then relentlessly attacks the ego as the ego stands for the disappointing object and the aggression felt towards the object is turned towards the ego, hence his description above that it is the ego in the melancholic that becomes poor and empty. Freud's description of the ego-destructive superego has been illustrated in recent years by several psychoanalysts working with manic-depressive patients (Bion, 1962; Lucas, 2004; O'Shaughnessy, 1999).

Although narcissistically withdrawn and pre-occupied with self-reproaches, the melancholic still maintains object relations, but the quality of these relations are often filled with hate and aggression.

> ... the patients usually still succeed, by the circuitous path of self-punishment, in taking revenge on the original object and in tormenting their loved one through their illness, having resorted to it in order to avoid the need to express their hostility to him openly. [Freud, 1917e, p. 251]

Freud believed melancholia runs its course and, when it comes to an end, the excess energy that was tied up in the internal struggle becomes free, which becomes the manic state.

Like Abraham, Klein (1935, 1940) felt that manic-depressive illness has its roots in infancy. In the path of psychic development the ego goes through positions of development and each position has as its hallmark a definitive set of anxieties and a constellation of defence mechanisms. Each position also brings forth different object relationships.

In the earlier paranoid–schizoid position, under the sway of projection, introjection, and splitting, an internal world is established, populated by extremely bad objects as well as perfect objects. The survival of the ego depends here on the annihilation of the bad object. As development proceeds, the internalization of good experiences and good objects will reassure the baby about its inner state and reduces the need to project. This implies that the baby will feel less threatened by objects made bad by his projections, which would imply that he would feel less aggressive towards his object. There will, hence, be a lesser need to split the ego or the object and so the ego becomes more integrated and the object, too, is experienced more as a whole object. In this way, the child sees the mother as both the loved object and, at other times, the hated object, and hence has ambivalent feelings towards her.

This is the onset of the depressive position. In this position, the child feels guilty for the aggressive feelings towards the object and also becomes aware that it does not possess her, and hence misses her and pines for her in her absence. It experiences the loss of the good object rather than the betrayal of a bad object. Because of the awareness of his guilt and concern for his object, the child develops the desire to repair the object.

If, however, the child's feelings towards the frustrating object are mostly hateful, the object will then not be missed but will be experienced as a bad object and is therefore reinstated in the internal world as a bad object. The inability to recover the loved object, and, more importantly, the loving feelings towards the object, is what Klein felt was underlying the melancholic state. The absence of an internal good object is what predisposes the individual later in life, in the face of object loss, to a melancholic state.

Mania

The superiority over the object and the freedom from the harshness of the internal tormenting object in the manic phase is expressed by Abraham, Freud, and Klein. In Freud's (1921c) writings on the ego-ideal, he described the change from melancholia to mania as the result of the ego's revolt against the ego-ideal. This rebellion is due to the ill-treatment the ego suffered in the hands of the ego-ideal in the melancholic phase.

Abraham (1924) similarly felt that the mania was the result of the triumph over the internal overbearing object. Abraham spoke about the manic patient presenting with an increase in oral desire, which is manifested not only in appetite for food: the manic patient devours everything that comes his or her way, as expressed in their increase in sexual desire and their rapid rate of speech. Similarly to the melancholic state, it represents an oral incorporation and expulsion of the loved object. He also thought that the manic state, like the melancholic state, worked itself out and that patients are only free to have relations to external objects once both phases have passed off.

Klein (1935, 1940) saw mania as a defence against the anxieties and despair provoked by the inability to protect the good object against hostile feelings. Like Freud and Abraham, she described the triumph over the object in the manic phase. Omnipotently filled with contempt and superiority, there is no concern for the fate of the object. The dependence on the relentless punishment from a severe internal object has been replaced by grandeur, where the manic patient feels *he has an abundance of everything and values nothing. He attacks his dependence on his objects and all their goodwill is destroyed.*

(Temperley, 2001). There is no guilt, and reparation is magical in that it does not acknowledge the damage, neither is there concern for the object.

Lucas (1998) illustrated in a case he analysed that the depressive phase represented a submission to a tyrannical superego and it was the rage resulting from this that fuelled the mania. He described how the manic phase could be viewed as the uncoiling of a clockwork spring that had been progressively tightened during the depressed phase. With regard to the cycles in the illness, he thought the resentment that builds up during the depressive phase fuelled the tightening spring, which then unwinds explosively during the manic phase. The unwinding continues until the anger is spent. Once the anger is spent, the pull to merge with the tyrannical superego returns.

Rey (1994) saw depression as the internalization of the destroyed object and the manic state as an identification with a magic penis which does not repair any damage, but acts to deny the damage done, similar to Klein's views on the presence of magical reparation phantasies in the manic phase.

In the European psychoanalytic literature, the melancholic phase is seen as the primary phase of manic-depressive states and the manic phase is seen as secondary to the psychic process which brought about the depressive phase. An opposing view has been described by some American psychoanalytic writers (Loeb & Loeb, 1987; Moore & Fine, 1968), who feel that the melancholic phase is secondary to the manic state, which is felt to be the primary disturbance. In their view, the manic state is the result of an increase in phallic instinctual drive that overwhelms the ego and the superego. They believe this increase in libido to be biologically determined. Melancholia, in their view, is due to the guilt caused by excessive sexual urges.

The theoretical understandings described above helped me in my understanding of my patient's illness and I hope to illustrate that below.

History

Shifa was referred for psychoanalysis by her psychiatric team. She has been suffering from manic-depressive illness for the past ten years. She started psychoanalysis with me three years ago and I see her five times a week on the couch. She is still under the treatment of her psychiatric team, and is presently on relatively high doses of antidepressants, antipsychotics, lithium, valproate, and thyroxine.

I vividly remember our first encounter. I noticed a dark figure standing in the street. There was something terribly slow about her movements, but there was more than that. I noticed her standing in front of my neighbours' house and staring into their window, making me feel slightly uncomfortable, as if my psychoanalytic practice is impinging upon the neighbourly boundaries. When their front door opened and she continued to stare, I realized there was something more than slow; there was something slightly odd about her. There was something blatantly intrusive, as well as a complete lack of awareness about her impact on the other.

Shifa is in her mid forties, a devout Muslim, living with her extended family. She is slow in her movements and carries her body as if it is a heavy burden. She wears traditional dark clothing most of the time, except when she has been manic, when her movements became fast and her clothes bright and colourful.

Shifa told me about a life that sounded painfully empty and tortured by the absence of life, activity, relationships, and anything else that gives meaning to one's daily existence. She felt herself unable to cope with the most basic tasks of daily living. She was completely unable to work. She would regularly not get out of bed for days on end and sometimes she would not be able care for herself physically.

As she painted the picture of a very bleak existence in my mind, I also heard the undertones of another picture where I became aware of the impact of her bleakness, withdrawal, and passivity on the family that was kindly looking after her. I started to get images of a passive, soundly asleep patient and, on the other hand, a furious household, tortured in their guilt for being angry with her and yet unable to understand or escape their fury. As an example, she described what appeared to be a remarkable aspect of her internal clock: it would wake her in perfect time for dinner each night, but when occasionally it was her turn to cook, she would oversleep and not wake up, leaving the others without food.

In her depressed phases, which have been dominant for the past three years, she withdrew herself to the inside of her bedroom, metaphorically much akin to the narcissistic withdrawal described in the analytic literature above, with the torturous impact on her loved ones illustrated in the preceding paragraph. Locked in her bedroom, she becomes the victim of devastating thoughts, leaving her feeling stupid, fat, useless, and totally unlovable; her only escape from this despair and terror is to sleep. She often reports that she has no thoughts. She seems to be stuck in a mental desert.

Contact with her in this state of mind is almost impossible, and the feeling of being with her brought forth uncomfortable experiences of irritation and hostility that were at times hard not to enact. I can feel resonance with her sense of being utterly ineffective, and it has made me wonder if this is what she felt like as a baby with her mother, feeling totally ineffective to rouse her mother's love.

In contrast, over the past three years there were times where she entered a hypo-manic phase, where her analysis livened up and she arrived like a spring flower in bright blossom. This brought with it a seduction to sit back and enjoy her lively flitting from one topic to the next. However, the danger of the reality of the manic phase was alarmingly clear with its omnipotence, grandeur, superiority, and the devouring nature Abraham and others so beautifully described. In this state of mind, her violence was no longer expressed passively, but enacted. Although on the surface she painted a floral picture filled with life, in my mind I heard the undertones of the anxiety those around her experienced, and indeed I experienced a great deal of it myself.

To give an example, in one of her manic breakdowns she left her washing in the machine for a few days, promising to take it out. One day her aunt exploded, and in her fury she emptied the washing machine, throwing Shifa's clothes on to the floor. The next minute Shifa jumped on her, threw her to the floor, and started beating her with her fists.

Her mania shores up all vulnerabilities. She is the source, aim, and object of her instincts. She feels she has everything, and when these omnipotent fantasies are threatened she has little by way of resources other than her violent rage.

Shifa told me the story of her troublesome younger life, which in a way tells a similar bleak tale, strongly reminding me of the views of Abraham and Klein that depression in adults has its roots in infancy.

She was the only child of her parents. Her early life was domi-nated by a lonely existence in a house where her mother was plagued by depression and her father was an alcoholic. In her black moods, her mother was explosive and unpredictable, leaving Shifa anxious and confused. She learned very quickly that safety meant a sacrifice of herself in favour of organizing her life around her mother's moods. Adapting her life around her mother's moods became so much the focus of her life that she had no other existence of her own; hence, she never formed friendships or relationships in her school years.

The dark shadows of a terrifying mother still loom in the back-ground of her mind, still infiltrating all relationships. As she told me about her current dependence on her family to care for her physically, I also became aware of their deep resentment towards her. It created an image in my mind of her as a tiny and helpless baby in the presence of a mother who was not only feeling dark and depressed, but resentful and hostile, providing "care" to her baby in a mechanical, loveless way and not with affection.

This reminds me of my first encounter with her, when I was so struck by her intrusive stares at my neighbour. Since then I have become very familiar with this stare, as she stares at me in a simi-lar way. It is as if the only way she knows about her safety is to stare at the face of another in order to try to enter into their mind to know whether she is going to be attacked or not. I think that such was the anxiety for her as a little girl that it had become the only way not to generate more hostility.

Unfortunately, for her there was no escape from this experience, as her father was mostly unavailable in her younger years due to his alcoholism, and he passed away when she was in her teens.

With her mind filled with anxiety and confusion, she found the challenges of academic work impossible, and hence did not complete her school career. Even in her adult years, I have noticed how the smallest of tasks or challenges makes her feel helpless and frightened and, in the face of these emotions, she gets thrown back unconsciously to an infantile state of terror which leaves her with a thinking apparatus in chaos.

Tragically, she has spent her adult life in this world of chaos, disorganization, and confusion, feeling panicked and lost. To defend herself from this inner terror, she tries to gain control of significant others by setting up a type of relationship in which she appears to be passive, yet she teases and tantalizes others to become engaged only in the end to behave in such a way that it leads to their frustration.

This, naturally, generates immense anger in others and leaves her surrounded with sadomasochistic interactions that one suspects she must somewhere find gratifying. This way of being long predates her depression. I would call this part of her character structure. Abraham and Klein felt depression has its roots in infancy; they both refer to a primary infantile depression, which I would imagine is what Shifa might have gone through as a baby, given my imagining of the absence of love she experienced. In her case, however, the presence of her infantile depression shaped the formation of her character, trapping her in infantile object relations for the rest of her life, never leaving her any escape from hate. It is this character structure that left her totally vulnerable to the depressive breakdowns she suffered in her adult life.

Breakdown

When Shifa was in her early thirties, a stranger followed her from the station and dragged her into a forest close to where she lived and raped her in broad daylight. She was terrified and feared that he would kill her. She described herself going into a state of frozen fear, unable to call for help or attempt to run away. She felt terrified, and was left with a deep sense of humiliation and shame afterwards. Several police interviews followed, and an identification parade, later followed by a court case, and the overwhelming shocked reactions of her family and local community. She went through these experiences dazed, in a state of dissociation, as if it were not real. Then, slowly, she became hypomanic. She became colourful in her clothing, cheerful and happy on the surface, and internally experienced an explosion of sexual libido and constant sexual fantasies of a sadomasochistic character. She got highly aroused indulging in fantasies of herself being sexually abused. These fantasies never left her, and each time she has had a manic or hypomanic breakdown since, her internal world becomes filled with the same fantasies. Abraham beautifully describes the insatiable hunger of the manic, which includes a hunger for sex so clearly illustrated in Shifa's material. Without any professional help, her hypomanic episode spontaneously settled after a short while.

A year after this traumatic episode, her mother suddenly died. Sadly, for Shifa, her dying mother was much the same mother she had known in infancy and for much of her life: cold, blaming, and unforgiving. With her mother's body being lowered into the ground, the shape of a dark, unforgiving, and torturous monster entered her mind and took centre stage in her inner world, subjecting her inner objects to a ruling dominated by cruelty. Shifa then had her first depressive breakdown, took to her bed, and withdrew herself from life, locked in a room of endless suffering and belief in her badness. There was no point in eating or in any form of living, and when eventually she felt suicide was the only way forward, psychiatric help was sought.

She was diagnosed with manic-depressive illness and started on medication which pulled her back from the brink, but she continued to live in an inner world dominated by the same constellations of object relations and the same anxiety about the state of her object, leaving her feeling disorganized and confused.

During her analysis in the past three years, she had one manic and one hypomanic episode, and several episodes of a deepening in her depression filled with total withdrawal and suicidal states. The analysis did help her each time to pull away from the brink, and perhaps the intensity and duration of her episodes became less than before the onset of her analysis. Mostly, the analysis helped her with her thinking, and the disorganization and chaos she can find herself in. I have noticed in her analysis that this state of inner chaos is utterly unbearable for her, and often her solution to free herself from this state is either to take manic flight or to contemplate suicide. Alternatively, she also creates order out of the chaos by setting up predictable object relations in which she experiences herself as a victim and feels unfairly treated by a persecutor.

Material from sessions

After she missed a session, she came to the next session saying she did not know whether I wanted to continue with her. She said she thought I would stop her analysis because she missed her session the day before. She simply slept through the time of her afternoon session and woke at 1.30 a.m. the next morning, thinking that it was time for her to get up for her session. She did not realize that it was in the middle of the night, and she went to have a shower. If it was not that her watch gave her the date, she would not have realized it was in the middle of the night.

I said she sounded as if she was feeling very confused, not knowing whether it was day or night, whether I wanted to see her or not. She said she had images and thoughts of cutting herself and taking all her tablets. She also had a dream. In her dream something seemed to have happened between her and her family, and the only solution she could see for herself was to jump into the toilet.

"The toilet is the place for shit, which is what my life is, I just can't go on.

"There is no other solution. I can't see how I will ever get better. Each time I fall down, it is impossible for me to get up. I just want to end it all. It is what I thought about yesterday all the time. It was almost as if I couldn't think about anything else."

I said she felt she messed things up between us and there was no way that it could be put right, and that made her feel her entire mind was a mess. She said, "It is a mess. Everything is a mess. Even when I speak I am told what comes out is rubbish.

"I feel hypersexed again. I think I am going high".

As she spoke I thought about her associations in the session. She came to her session expecting to find me enraged at her, unforgiving and punishing her for the missed session. The analytic relationship in her mind seems to have been damaged beyond repair by her missing the session the day before. Now, all she seems to expect from me is relentless punishment. The punishment, however, seems to have been a state of mind she was trapped in which predated the session, as she spent the previous day filled with fantasies of cutting herself to pieces, which in the end led to her cutting out her session. This violent onslaught of relentless hate and unforgiveness, as well as her confusional state of mind, expressed in her inability to differentiate between night and day, brought to my mind the image of a resentful, hostile mother holding a baby filled with confusion and terror. I thought about Freud's clear description of the identification with the object, and how the relentless fury against the disappointing object is taken out on the ego. This is illustrated in her dream where she is in a relentless argument with her family and no repair seems possible, reason gets reduced to chaos and confusion. Her attempt to free herself from the inner tormentor seems to be one of two possible solutions: to destroy the object with suicide, or to go into manic flight where the object is obliterated and she is reinstated as the source and aim of her desires, hence her feeling hypersexed.

I found myself feeling anxious, aware of an impulsive pressure present in her, and from experience I knew that the pressure would push her to act—much like jumping into the toilet to get away from the unbearable internal state. I wondered what I could say that could be helpful, especially as I knew from experience how difficult it is for her to understand anything I say when she is in a confused state of mind. Then suddenly I thought about her capacity to notice her manic state, and I realized that this capacity was evidence of a saner part of her that could observe herself in a realistic way.

I decided to try to make contact with this non-psychotic part of her by saying that there was a part of her mind that was not confused, and it was able to notice that she was trying to find frightening solutions such as suicide or mania to get away from unbearable feelings inside her. She agreed, and said she thought she should go to the emergency psychiatric clinic. I said there seemed to be a sensible part of her that was aware she needed help; that was the part that brought her to her session and the part that thought she needed to see her psychiatrist. After the session, she contacted her psychiatric team.

She arrived for the next session saying she had a conversation with a friend, but something happened and it became a mess and the friend became angry and upset with her. She wanted to take all her pills, but then thought she should phone the helpline. Then she thought she was not feeling that bad and did not need to phone.

Then she thought again that she should just take all her pills and go to sleep.

I saw this as a similar sequence to the day before. I decided to be more robust and took up her destructiveness. I said "When you do what you've just done, you play Russian roulette with your life and with me and it makes you feel all powerful."

"What am I supposed to do then?" she said, "Just do it and not tell you, because if I tell you, you think I do it to you?"

I said, "You feel very accused by me, as if you want me not to analyse what you say." She responded with a furious silence. I commented that I thought I had made her angry with what I said.

She said, "You slapped me in the face. It was like with my friend.

"Things were OK in the beginning and then it went all wrong. I don't remember what you said any more. I didn't hear you and the next minute you fired guns."

I said, "Let's go back and see what happened. You spoke about wanting to take your pills and not wanting to take them, as if you were playing a game with your life."

"Yes, I remember," she said.

I said, "Then I said that you were playing Russian roulette with yourself and with me and that it made you feel very powerful. That is when you got angry."

"Yes," she said.

I said, "And I think it made you angry because somewhere inside you, you realized you were doing something provocative and that it made you feel powerful. You didn't want to see that and you didn't want me to see that, and that is why you wanted me to shut up."

"It is a dangerous game I suppose," she said.

I said, "When you feel powerful like that it helps you to feel less confused. But it is a dangerous game as it threatens the very relationships you value and that makes you feel bad and more confused."

She thought about it for a while, and then said, "I was actually beginning to collect my pills."

"Telling me that means that you feel I am a helpful person again and you can bring the side of you to me which can be destructive to you."

She came back for the next session less suicidal, saying she had started taking her medication again and she felt a bit better. She had been able to get up in the morning and completed a few tasks. "Trouble is, what about next week?" she said.

I said she was feeling more hopeful today, but worried things would become messed up again.

This is what analysis is like with her at the moment; the close relationship with me is at times life saving, but it also weaves itself into her illness and becomes a threat to her life. There are times, moments really, when I am able to make contact with the non-psychotic part of her, by which I mean the part that is struggling against the chaos and confusion in her mind. At other times the psychotic and confused part predominates, be it on a high tide or a low tide. At these moments the transference becomes the madness, and helping her move out of that state of mind is dangerous for both her and me. Making her responsible for the impact of her actions on those trying to help her was such a moment. Showing her my experience of her as at the receiving end of her partially loaded gun in this instance helped her to come back from a brink. I am not grandiose enough to expect that this will be the case every time. Yet, contrary to the expectations of many, she is alive, and I am also here to tell you her tale.

Discussion

I want now to provide some speculations about the nature of Shifa's illness and, in particular, to consider its dramatic onset: the hypomania after the rape and her depressive breakdown after her mother's death. I think these formative moments of her life help us a little in understanding the complex way illness as a process unfolds and takes over the mind, and perhaps studying this might inspire us to think of effective ways of preventing, or even reversing, these processes.

Given her hypomanic state after the rape, one can hypothesize that the fragile balance of her symbolic capacity collapsed and consequently she experienced the rape as an actualization of a fantasized incestuous victory over an overbearing mother. The fantasy becoming real opened a door that stopped the communication of fantasy and reality. Once the door was opened, she was vulnerable to the experience, happenings in the real word directly triggering consequences at the level of unconscious fantasy. This would explain her triumphant state and also her depressive collapse when her mother died, which she must have experienced as due to her unconscious phantasies as to the damage her mother did to her. Then, a melancholic situation set in, with the overbearing mother being internalized and the subsequent sadomasochistic internal relationship coming starkly into effect.

Except for manic periods in which she is temporarily released from this captured state, my patient never recovers from the devouring nature of this deep-rooted internal object relationship, predicated on her perception of her relationship with her mother. The psychotic process takes hold again and again, and is in control of processing her experience, bringing unconscious fantasy into the world of the everyday relationship. In her case, the manic-depressive illness has the malignancy it has possibly because it is a repetition of her earlier life experience, where she sacrificed her life to submit to the unpredictability of a tyrannical mother. Without having an oedipal father, or any significant others who could rescue her from this difficult dyadic relationship, it meant there were very few protective factors to provide alternative protective internal good objects.

The omnipresence of such an internal persecutor understandably gave rise to high levels of anxiety when she was a child. Such anxiety would have led to her using primitive defensive mechanisms to cope. In turn, such mechanisms would have led to further weakening of her ego, and hence the propensity towards fragmentation. When the psychotic break occurs, there is nothing there for my patient to help her to hold back the onslaught of the urgent demands of unconscious fantasy for actualization. Freud (1900a) and Sandler and Sandler (1998) referred to this as identity of perception: creating an identity between an internal state of affairs and an external one to achieve gratification of the internal state.

In other words, what has become clear in treating Shifa is the temporal unfolding of the psychological aspect of manic depressive illness. It is clear that, both experientially and biologically, my patient was constantly at risk throughout her development. She obviously managed to stay clear of trouble by dramatically curtailing her exposure to the social world and the need to understand people, but, perhaps even more importantly in her case, the risk of interactions triggered a catastrophic psychological reaction. Living an asexual existence, developing no friendships or important attachments, could be seen as a prodromal symptom, but in her case is better understood as the rational response of a woman who recognized that the barrier separating her unconscious fantasies from social reality was fragile, too fragile to be tested in the daily hassle and bustle of interchange between self and others.

The clinical material that emerged from her treatment makes it abundantly clear that the fantasy of her early oedipal resistances being literally overpowered by an external male agency were there as part of the dynamic of her relationship with her mother and father. She was not to be permitted to have a genital relationship, but if it were forced on her, she would comply. The fantasy was deeply unconscious, but made real by the experience of rape. Were she not biologically susceptible to the experience of an actualization of an unconscious fantasy, she is likely to have survived the attack with perhaps an episode of PTSD. However, the unconscious becoming conscious in conjunction with the biological weakness in her ego's capacity to process symbolic material forced her to abandon the ways of coping in reality that we generally consider to be within our socially acceptable limits. In her reaction to the rape, she merged with what must have been a very early representation of an idealized father figure created by her mind to cope with maternal unavailability and explicit rejection. Sadomasochism, in her case, seems to have been part of her personality structure prior to the onset of the illness, which I think she used as a defence against fragmentation, probably even before the onset of the psychosis. When this figure became part of her reality, not just an unconscious fantasy, she went mad.

Her madness was aggravated when her maternal superego, a far from benign persecutory rejecting fantasy, also became real and turned against her. These events have set a psychotic process into motion that she had been bravely fighting throughout her young adult life, but was now overpowered by. Social experiences could no longer be reliably separated from unconscious fantasies. She was the victim of her internal world, a place of little love and much persecution. We have already tried to understand her reaction to various transference and extra-transference events in terms of her attempt to reduce the confusional state that the very reality of her unconscious fantasies creates for her. Her skin needs rigid unmovable structures to protect it, and obviously, if they are going to shift at all, it will be only after many more years of treatment. However, the formulation above gives a clear goal to our analytic work. Understanding the unconscious fantasies that are in any case too real for her is not a major or necessarily helpful part of our work. What seemed far more helpful were the episodes of the kind I described above, where our work could focus on the nature of her thinking and the way in which her uncontrollable emotions and beliefs of delusional force might lead her to self-destruction.

Conclusion

In this presentation, I have attempted to illustrated the complex interplay between what could be considered a diagnosable "mental illness" and my patient's internal experiences. The literature conveys how both phases of the illness repeatedly come and go. Some patients suffering from the condition lead relatively rewarding and successful lives. Perhaps their early life experiences enabled their personalities to be more integrated. The actualization of unconscious fantasy would perhaps have been more bearable for my patient if her internal objects had been benign in her unconscious fantasy life and in the actual attachment history that created the unconscious world. My patient's early deprivation is, I think, significant. I have highlighted how painfully unrewarding her life can feel and how, inevitably, this can also be felt in her treatment. Of course, we should not ignore the possibility that it is not just experience that creates unconscious fantasy, but biological predisposition, including aggression, emotional regulation, and impulsivity that make a contribution to how the care-taking world is experienced by the infant and young child. But that makes life even more complicated than my patient and I have already made it!

Acknowledgements

Special thanks to Peter Fonagy and Richard Lucas, who helped me with my thoughts about the paper.

References

Abraham, K. (1911). Manic-depressive insanity. In: *Selected Papers of Karl Abraham* (pp. 137–157). New York: Basic Books, 1953.

Abraham, K. (1924). A short study of the development of the libido, viewed in the light of developmental disorders. In: *Selected Papers of Karl Abraham* (pp. 93–109). London: Hogarth.

Bion, W. (1962). *Learning From Experience*. London: Karnac.

Farmer, A., Eley, T. C., & McGuffin, P. (2005). Current strategies for investigating the genetic and environmental risk factors for affective disorders. *British Journal of Psychiatry, 186*(3): 179–181.

Fenichel, O. (1945). *The Psychoanalytic Theory of Neurosis.* New York: Norton.

Freud, S. (1900a). *The Interpretation of Dreams. S.E.,* 5: 509–610. London: Hogarth.

Freud, S. (1917e). Mourning and melancholia. *S.E.,* 14: 237–259. London: Hogarth.

Freud, S. (1921c). *Group Psychology and the Analysis of the Ego. S.E., 18:* 67–143. London: Hogarth.

Haldane, M., & Frangou, S. (2004). New insights helped define pathophysiology of bipolar affective disorder: neuroimaging and neuropathology findings. *Progress in Neuro-psychopharmacology and Biological Psychiatry, 28*(6): 943–960.

Jacobson, E. (1971). *Depression.* New York: International Universities Press.

Klein, M. (1935). A contribution to the psychogenesis of manic-depressive states. In: *Writings of Melanie Klein, 1:* 262–289. London: Hogarth.

Klein, M. (1940). Mourning and its relation to manic-depressive states. In: *Writings of Melanie Klein, 1:* 344–369. London: Hogarth.

Loeb, F. F., & Loeb, R. L. (1987). Psychoanalytic observations on the effect of lithium on manic attacks. *Journal of American Psychoanalytic Association, 35:* 877–902.

Lucas, R. (1998). Why the cycle in cyclical psychosis? An analytic contribution to the understanding of recurrent manic-depressive psychosis. *Psychoanalytic Psychotherapy, 12*(3): 193–212.

Lucas, R. (2004). The management of depression—analytic, antidepressants or both? *Psychoanalytic Psychotherapy, 18*(3): 268–284.

McGuffin, P., Rijdsdijk, F., Andrew, M., Sharm, P., Katz, R., & Cardro, A. (2003). The heritability of bipolar affective disorder and the genetic relationship to unipolar depression. *Archives of General Psychiatry, 60:* 497–502.

Moore, B., & Fine, B. (1968). *A Glossary of Psychoanalytic Terms and Concepts.* New York: American Psychoanalytical Association.

O'Shaughnessy, E. (1999). Relating to the superego. *International Journal of Psychoanalysis, 80:* 861–870.

Rey, H. (1994). *Universals of Psychoanalysis in the Treatment of Psychotic and Borderline States.* London: Free Association.

Sandler, J., & Sandler, A. (1998). *Internal Objects Revisited.* London: Karnac.

Savitz, J., Solms, M., & Rajkumar, R. (2005). Neuropsychological dysfunction in bipolar affective disorder: a critical opinion. *Bipolar Disorders, 7*(3): 216–235.

Temperley, J. (2001). The depressive position. In: *Kleinian Theory: A Contemporary Perspective*. London: Whurr.

CHAPTER SIX

Response to the chapter by Trudie Rossouw on manic-depression

Richard Lucas

I n 1916, Freud bemoaned the absence of an analytic presence in general psychiatry, commenting, "Our psychiatrists are not students of psychoanalysis and we psycho-analysts see too few psychiatric patients". He hoped that the situation would be rectified in the USA (Freud 1916–1917).

Within this context, Trudie Rossouw's thoughtful and thought-provoking presentation of live material is very much to be welcomed. An opportunity arises to consider the role that analytic thinking has to offer in the area of bipolar affective disorder or recurrent manic-depressive states.

At an organic level, we still remain in the dark about the aetiology of major psychotic disorders. We rely heavily for our bearings at the clinical descriptive level. What we know for a fact is that in some cases all interventions, including mood stabilizers, have a very limited effect, and the episodes become more protracted with increasing age rather than improving.

This can be a soul-destroying experience for analysts, and might account for why so few cases are reported in the analytic literature, yet it is no bad thing that one's delusions of omnipotence and

81

cherished beliefs are shattered and that we are forced to think again about what might be happening.

As Dr Rossouw points out, analytic observations allow us to observe the recurrent process in a unique way as it unfolds within the patient's inner world. To give you a brief vignette of how longitudinal, analytically based observations can be applied within the general psychiatric context, an NHS patient in her early sixties was transferred to my care. I noted at the time that she was on many medications, including a depot and two mood stabilizers, and I concluded that she must be attributing magical properties to medication to rid herself of sanity and feelings.

When she developed mild renal impairment, we had to stop the Lithium, as it was reaching dangerously high levels. Her family observed that she reacted as if we had taken away her lover. It resulted in a protracted admission. First, she went high, but in a quiet, smiling way, walking with mincing steps like playing grandmother's footsteps, but, every now and then, hitting another patient without warning. It was as if she reacted to the loss of the idealized God/Lover/Lithium by manically becoming the ideal and hitting other patients as if they were trying to steal this from her.

Later followed a period of retribution, as if coming down on her from a jealous God whose role she had attempted to take over. She talked of hell and damnation, the end of the world, thunderbolts from heaven, and would sleep under the bed to protect herself from harm. It took a full nine months for her to recover her equilibrium. Leaving aside those who would attribute the manic-depressive episode entirely to a biochemical cause, carrying with one an analytic perspective allows one to follow the progress of the psychotic journey, as Dr Rossouw suggests.

Another interesting question raised by Dr Rossouw is: can analysis alter the intensity of the storms and render them less dangerous? One response might be that it depends on the intransigence of the psychopathology.

I learned this lesson only too well from a patient with recurrent manic-depression, whom I saw analytically for many years in the Health Service (Lucas, 1998). At one point, in a severely manic state, she had to be managed on the intensive care unit. She had stripped to her underwear and was excitedly idealizing associating with all psychopaths in the hospital. I pointed out how she seemed to have lost all contact with her caring objects, her husband and myself. She appeared visibly moved by this, and said as she was leaving the session, "Thank you." She left, then put her head back round the door and said, "But, no thanks!" (Lucas, 1998).

From prolonged contact with such a patient, while I was unable to make an impact on her recurrent manic episodes, I formed the view that her mania was a rebellion against a tyrannical superego to which she submitted in her depressive phases. She was unable to stop the manic rebellious outpouring once started. I learned an important lesson: to respect a part of herself, which was having to manage the situation. Perhaps, linked to sharing my analytic interest with the nursing staff, they also developed a respect for the patient and accepted when the patient said that she was ready to leave the ward and manage her mania back in the community.

In patients with less severe and intransigent episodes, one can make more of an impact, and this can be particularly important in the area of suicide, where bipolar affective disorders can carry up to a 15% risk of suicide.

A patient whom I heard about in supervision experienced both manic phases, where she identified with being God's servant, and deadly depressive phases, where she kept a rope in the loft with the intent to hang herself, as she felt that she was allowed no life of her own by her demanding internal objects and would exact her revenge.

By mobilizing a separate, reflective part of herself, she became fearful of the creeping up on her of a deadly self-destructive state of mind. She reported a dream of stealth bombers depositing their deadly load, and started to become interested in, and reflective over, her psychopathology. As a result, later in her treatment she was able to say to her therapist that she was now able to allow herself to have longings and it did not seem so important whether she actually got them or not (Taylor-Thomas & Lucas, 2006).

I report this material not only to balance with more positive therapeutic experiences the reporting of more intransigent cases and encourage a continued analytic presence in this most difficult of areas, but also to consider Dr Rossouw's other key point: how do we make an impact on the patient? In fact, Dr Rossouw gives us a convincing illustration of the technique she used to make an impact on her patient in her reported sessional material.

In order to make an impact in psychosis, we have to develop a particular approach, to which Bion gave us the key when he talked of the operation of two separate parts to the personality in major psychotic disorders (Bion, 1957). The psychotic part cannot think, but acts as a muscular organ to evacuate thoughts arrived at by work of the non-psychotic part. In manic depression, the psychotic part is dominated by a deadly drive for an omnipotent fusion with God and treats sanity, as advocated through the non-psychotic part, as its life-long rival. Hence, even when Dr Rossouw's patient acknowledged progress made in a session, she added, "Trouble is, what about next week?", but at least it was less severe than my patient's response of "Thanks but no thanks!"

I would go further than Abraham, who saw the onset of the psychopathology occurring pre-oedipally in the early relationship with the mother, and suggest that the patient emerges from the womb with a predominating psychotic part searching for identification with a god-like breast rather than a good-enough mother (Abraham, 1924). In that sense, though typically in manic-depression there is an emotionally unavailable mother with a highly pronounced depression, as in Dr Rossouw's case, the pull from the beginning is to want to identify with such an object as representing an idealized mechanical relationship devoid of feelings. Hence, the more human father was sidelined.

I would, therefore, see the underlying psychopathology in Dr Rossouw's patient as present from the beginning of life, with the question being what precipitated the manic-depressive mood swings. The rape, on its own, does not. It appears predominantly to result in her becoming more excited over the sadistic triumphant raping of her non-psychotic part. What causes the problem is the separation from the absolute identification with the omnipotent mother figure, with her mother's death. Now she is born for the first time in terms of a conflict between the wish to continue to remain with the deadly identification and a non-psychotic part, with its interest in thinking and life.

In this context, one is always looking for the destructive functioning of the psychotic part, which might disguise itself, inviting one to treat the patient as if we were dealing with a neurotic disorder. As the psychotic part tends to disown awareness through projection, the countertransference provides important information as to what is happening. Hence, Dr Rossouw's vivid description of at times feeling the patient stuck in a mental desert, at other times feeling the frustration of a sadistic control, being driven mad, while at other times swept along by the omnipotent mania. So, Dr Rossouw concludes that "it is almost impossible to make and maintain contact with her". Yet, remarkably, she does maintain that contact in the reported session.

The relevance of looking at the presented material in terms of a conflict between two separate parts, the psychotic and non-psychotic, is apparent from the beginning. When the patient over-sleeps and misses a session, the non-psychotic part invites one to consider the reason. The psychotic part responds, first by sadistically attacking potential meaning, and then disguising the attack by creating confusion. The psychotic part then advocates jumping into the shit in the toilet, with threats that impulsively she might commit suicide.

Dr Rossouw decided first to try to make contact with the patient's non-psychotic reflective part. One minute it appeared to help and the patient thought of seeing her psychiatrist for helpful pills to contain her destructive mania, but this attitude did not last and she returned the next day reporting that she was thinking of taking all her pills.

Dr Rossouw then decided to be more robust and actively confront the psychotic part and take up the destructiveness. At first the patient turned it into an accusation, saying that Dr Rossouw had slapped her in the face. In manic states, patients often twist things round through using the defence mechanism of projection and reversal into the opposite. Dr Rossouw impressively held firm, went over what had happened with the patient, and helped her to see in clear terms how being powerful helped her to feel less confused but threatened the relationship that she values with the therapist. The patient was able to acknowledge this, resulting in her returning to taking her medication and becoming less suicidal.

In Dr Rossouw's patient, the wish for constructive help with her difficulties is apparent, much more than in the patient I was seeing, even if any progress is open to be swept away by further tidal destructive forces, which is the penalty of being involved with such patients.

With regard to an underlying theme of contrasting the organic with the inner world, I find it is interesting to return to the consideration of the possibility that an attitude of mind may be present from birth in manic-depression, with searching for the preconception of idealized god-like object innately being stronger than for the preconception of a good-enough breast mother. Of course, how the mother actually relates must either reinforce or mitigate this dominating phantasy.

If looked at from this point of view, then we do not have to maintain psychoanalytic conflicts between diehard Kleinians and diehard Winnicottians as to whether the internal phantasy world or the external environmental object relationships are more significant, as both will play their parts in manic-depression. Neither do we have to be in conflict between the general psychiatric (in terms of genetics, biochemistry, and the responsiveness to medication) and psychotherapeutic approaches, as all have their contributory aspects.

The following vignette illustrates this. An elderly widow was referred to me for guidance. Her son had developed severe manic episodes. He lacked insight, became aggressive in manner, and went wandering off in France. When he returned, he lived with his mother in the countryside. The response from the local psychiatric service had so far been very limited. I had been asked to discuss whether psychoanalytic psychotherapy could help as an alternative to conventional psychiatry, as the patient was making no progress. The mother was, in fact, employing the right strategy. When he became ill in a manic way, he demanded his passport. She said that she had mislaid it and that she was looking for it, but actually phoned his brother to come round and help.

She found it helpful to have feedback that her action was totally appropriate, that he posed a difficult management problem, and the need was to get full involvement of the psychiatric service, with his being placed on an enhanced care programme approach. Any issue of whether psychotherapy may be available through the local psychology service or otherwise could wait, and only be considered in the light of first establishing an overall effective containment and support for the mother, through the local psychiatric services.

Facing up to the management of manic-depressive states truly invites a synthesis of the organic and the inner world, and Dr

Rossouw's presentation has truly provided such an opportunity for reflection in this challenging area.

References

Abraham, K. (1924). A short study of the development of libido. In: *Selected Papers on Psychoanalysis*. London: Karnac, 1988.
Bion, W. R. (1957). Differentiation of the psychotic from the non-psychotic personalities. In: *Second Thoughts*. London: Karnac, 1984.
Freud, S. (1916–1917). *Introductory Lectures on Psycho-Analysis*. S.E., 16: 412–430.
Lucas, R. (1998). Why the cycle in a cyclical psychosis? An analytic contribution to the understanding of recurrent manic-depressive psychosis. *Psychoanalytic Psychotherapy, 12*: 193–212.
Taylor-Thomas, C., & Lucas, R. (2006). Consideration of the role of psychotherapy in reducing the risk of suicide in affective disorders—a case study. *Psychoanalytic Psychotherapy, 20*: 218–234.

CHAPTER SEVEN

Where is the unconscious in dementia?

Sandra Evans

An old lady sits in a chair next to a large picture mirror. She responds to the visiting psychiatrist's question about loneliness. No, she never gets lonely. She eats her lunch every day with the lady next door. Her meals on wheels are delivered daily at about midday. She seems cheerful, but is very forgetful and confused. The psychiatrist realizes that "the lady next door" is the patient's own, unrecognized reflection in the mirror. Her composure and self-containment allow her to remain at home despite grave disability.

An elderly man is seen at home for an urgent assessment. He has begun to attack windows and mirrors at home. Whenever he sees his reflection, he fails to recognize himself and defends himself against a perceived malign intruder. His paranoid aggression presents a risk. He is a danger to himself and others, and consequently he is hospitalized.

Both patient examples are drawn from ordinary clinical practice in old age psychiatry. Both suffered from prosopagnosia; an inability to recognize one's own mirror image. This is caused by bilateral lesions in the central visual system; in the medial occipito-temporal regions (Damasio, Damasio, & Van Hoesen, 1982). While other lesions might have accounted for the differences between their responses, and on a strictly scientific level we have to consider that as a distinct possibility, it might be interesting to explore other possible explanations. Fleminger (1992) proposed that our expectations prejudice our perceptions; the products of our psyche influences how we see things. Furthermore, this can be fuelled by misidentification syndromes. Fleminger was referring to schizophrenia, but his thesis pertains just as well for dementia. In the above scenarios, then, the misidentification syndrome caused by brain lesions has produced very different results clinically. The product of the individual patients' internal worlds is projected unconsciously on to their every day surroundings. This then has a consequence for the type of experience they have during illness.

As people dement, they do so in unique ways; in part due to myriad constellations of brain lesions in the degenerative brain disorders. The degenerating brains belong to people, whose *minds* are the result of an even greater variety of genetic inheritance and life experiences. It is the personality and their experience of the life lived which further enriches work with this group of individuals. Knight (1986) suggests that people become more themselves, more obviously different from others and their cohort as they age. Perhaps generally older people have a stronger sense of "core self" than younger adults. This may be a protective factor in a dementing illness, and may explain why, despite extreme illness, many elderly people seem to respond in idiosyncratic ways .

Using object relations theory to analyse the clinical illustrations above, one might speculate on the internal object relations of these two people. In the first are benign introjections, self-objects, using Kohutian definitions, or a good-enough introjected mother, using a Winnicottian view. The message is similar: the old lady has herself to be with. That self is experienced as a friendly, supportive "neighbour". The man, by contrast, is persecuted by the projections of his mind, and feels under attack and in need of violent self-defence. Melanie Klein would recognize this as the paranoid–schizoid position, demonstrated and truly acted out in front of our eyes. The notion that the loss of certain parts of the mind contributes to an absence of reality-testing, with resultant re-emergence of primary process thinking and the rekindling of repressed unconscious material, is the basis of my essay. I will speculate on the processes that we observe, the experience communicated to us by our patients, and the value of this to our patients.

Communication in dementia

The brain damage that occurs in dementia, is an immense challenge to sufferers and to the people supporting them and working with them. When dementia is in an advanced state, verbal communication is often compromised, which adds to feelings of frustration and sometimes despair. Non-verbal communication by means of projective identification is very common. This is experienced mainly by people's most intimate carers, not always relatives, but often poorly paid workers, many of whom are women. The carers' own life experiences with child-rearing may assist them with coping and understanding the needs of the people with dementia, as demonstrated by Haggstrom and Norberg (1996).

It must be emphasized that people with dementia are not children or small babies. Even though a psychoanalytic framework based on infant development is helpful to us in thinking about needs, feelings, and behaviour, they are very different in terms of the state of their minds, compared with the very young, whose minds are still developing. Their years of life do add a richness to their mental lives that distinguishes them particularly from babies and young children, although the memories and fantasies and current mental life may well be experienced in the same timeless fashion of unconscious processes. In addition, there will be islands of memory, and a sense of coherent personhood, even if the coherence is experienced in the past tense. This demands dignified expression of self and an acknowledgement of status gained and earned.

The special conditions of unconscious mental life in dementia

What many people with dementia lose quite early on in the illness is the ability to reality-test. For this reason, delusional ideas can arise in people who have never previously suffered a psychotic illness, and, to some extent, primary process thinking becomes the norm. Anything might happen. One might be the daily victim of petty crime, even by carers, who are believed to have stolen anything that is unaccounted for, in a defensive move against the knowledge and shame of losing one's mind. One's dead mother can be waiting for one at the end of a day at the day centre, as though that person were still coming home from school. It is often the distress and upset of this early separation re-experienced in late adult life that institutional carers are responding to when they attempt to reassure "Mrs Jones". An empathic carer may respond in a strong maternal way to imploring about wanting "to go home". It is their wish to soothe that compels them to join in with the fantasy that mother is alive and that she will soon be home. How harsh it seems to remind Mrs Jones that her mother died decades ago; instead, she has a husband and grown up children who might visit later. It is this aspect of unconscious communication that dominates the world of people with dementia; one that is laden with affects. Self-reflection, plumbing the depths of one's own feelings as carer, is often the key to understanding the world of dementia.

In order to illustrate the omnipresent nature of unconscious processes, an example from a colleague's observation in a continuing care unit for people with severe dementia is offered. The reporter was particularly sensitive, and quick to get to know the characters in the home.

> I feel somewhat down, bored and depressed in the room today. There is no activity. Nellie refuses to walk to dance/movement group and just wants to sit in her chair. I feel very tired and listless. I am aware that I am stressed and somewhat physically tired myself, but that does not account for the feelings of lassitude that overcome me today in the room. Is it because the residents are physically unwell with their infections; are they more bored than usual? Apart from the lack of music in the room, there is not much difference. Perhaps it is that today the carers are not spending time in the room. When they are there, they talk among themselves and sometimes directly to the residents. Even their conversations somehow animate the room and normally fend off this feeling of boredom and exhaustion that has seemed to develop when there is no one here apart from the residents.

What is particularly fascinating about this account of self-reflection is how the speaker has counted himself in with the residents and no longer identifies as a carer or observer. The feelings of lassitude and boredom are overwhelming. This appears to be a most powerful projective identification. There seems nothing to fill conscious life and nothing to spark a memory or even a fantasy.

How does speculating on the mental life of a person who is losing their mind assist us in our understanding of patient's experience? It is clearly important to recognize that mental activity does continue, even if pondering on the experience is uncomfortable. Certainly, improvements in the understanding of the feelings of people who can no longer express their wishes verbally has resulted in enhanced quality of care and important changes to the physical care environment. Homes for people with dementia are no longer "warehouses", and the best examples of care are often lively environments where people are treated with kindness and empathy.

Using observation techniques developed by Esther Bick (1986), Rustin (1989) and McKenzie-Smith (1992) began observing elderly people in institutional settings and from a psychoanalytic as well as sociological perspective. The Tavistock clinic has now been teaching these techniques for some considerable time to clinicians working with older patients. Useful and moving clinical papers have emerged which alert us to the value of understanding countertransference and projective identifications in clinical work with people with dementia, not only to understand better the needs of patients, but in order to contain our own feelings of dread and disgust. Margot Waddell (2000) made sense of an elderly woman's intolerance of separation, and Davenhill, Balfour, Rustin, and Blanchard (2003) demonstrated how reflective practice in care home settings can usefully reduce the inadvertent neglect of people's needs.

Attempts to understand through empathy another's experience is arguably the most important aspect of our humanity. It prevents us from allowing such people to become the repository of our negative projections, our own unconscious, and also dilutes the unwanted and disavowed parts of our own psyche. It protects them from our unconscious attacks, as Garner and Evans (2001) point out in a report designed to raise awareness of unconscious processes in abusive behaviour in institutional settings.

It is perhaps an unconscious protective mechanism at work in carers that underlies the drive not to communicate effectively with people with dementia. Anxiety about our own future old age causes us to ignore their communications, which are slowed or altered by disease, but are present, none the less. Kitwood (1988) and Menzies Lyth (1959) have cited negative personal, social, and institutional unconscious actions, which further impair those with dementia while "protecting" the sensibilities of carers. This effect is not limited to professional carers in homes, but also seems to occur in peers frightened by witnessing others' deterioriation.

An interesting observation came from an untrained but experienced worker in supportive accommodation for frail elderly people, few with dementia. The non-demented residents tended to operate a scapegoat system towards the most "feeble-minded" of individuals. In this arena, where most residents are elderly and often in fear of losing their minds, the demented person is singled out and cast apart from the rest of the community. The residents seemed to find dementia particularly difficult to bear, and yet none would see themselves individually as having anything against that person. This particular group dynamic is not uncommon, as described by Golander and Raz (1996) and might include some envy of the special status of people with dementia who are allowed the freedom not to conform. Evans (1998) borrowed the term "malignant mirroring" from the late Louis Zinkin to describe the difficulties of getting older people into groups together, caused by the negative projective identification. They are "full of old people", and the fear that they are demented too adds to the anxiety that it may be catching.

Ploton (1995) offers descriptions of people's behaviour, the islands of memory, and transient normal functioning as evidence of continued mental activity. He suggests that this unconscious life remains, no matter how demented a person becomes. The idea of unconscious mental life in dementia was put forward as early as the 1930s (Grotjahn, 1938). Thinking and feeling are two linked aspects of mental life. A great deal of feeling apparently continues, even in very advanced or end-stage dementia. We are not so clear about the amount and quality of the thinking in someone with end-stage dementia who lies supine, with apparently unseeing eyes and no recognizable purposeful movements. Such people still utter sounds, and convey affect and pain, common human emotions.

Some aspects of mental functioning that are essential to life include the mechanism that allows us to breathe. Without the apparatus of our brainstem we would not be able to do this. We are aware of our breathing only when we are unable to do it. The medulla, or brainstem, is part of the more primitive aspects of our brain, one that on an evolutionary level is similar in all mammals and demonstrates the automatic feature of a great deal of mental functioning. The awareness of this functioning or its absence, however, is the domain of the cortex (arguably), the part of the brain that degenerates in Alzheimer's disease. We can remain alive, breathing and with a continued heartbeat, while all higher functions are gone. If we lose all the cortical parts of our brain, this appears to correspond to the end of unconscious life too. Physicians turn off life support only after multiple tests have been performed, including electro-encephalogram to diagnose "brain death". This is qualitatively different from people with dementia, whose EEG's are still active, though slowed and changed in ways characteristic of neuro-degenerative disorders. People with dementia, a neuro-degenerative process that can deteriorate slowly over many years, experience their mental life as changed, not over.

Some authors have turned to dementia in order to understand dreaming. They have likened the loss of reality testing in dementia to the unconscious processing that occurs during dreams. The similarities cited are the co-existence of dead and living people within the same time frame and the lack of need for logic, among other things. Some patients in a dementing state find it difficult to differentiate between dreams and reality, as is shown in the vignette below.

> A patient reported having been broken into in her flat, and having all her important documents stolen from her, particularly her passport and bank details.
>
> In fact she had not been burgled, but had been disturbed during the night, as reported by her husband. He had seen her get up out of bed and, while still sleeping, she had rifled through her chest of drawers as though looking for something.

It is not hard to imagine this woman's unspoken fear of losing her identity along with other important personal details. This particular dream continued after she woke; clearly, the feeling stayed with her. One might conjecture that her confabulation about the burglary was her making sense of her powerfully retained dream, and her unconscious sense of herself disappearing.

In dementia there is often, but not always, an awareness of the loss of memory. This is undoubtedly linked to the progressive and then sometimes diminishing levels of anxiety experienced by people with an awareness of a progressive loss of personal resources. Depending on their early, "unremembered" experiences of infancy and early childhood from the care-giving point of view, they may experience more or less anxiety and depression during the process. This view of Martindale's describes for us in exquisite detail the role of the unconscious phantasy of abandonment, or of a persecutory dependence on others. The individual is unaware of the past, deeply repressed in the unconscious, but experiences dread at the loss of independence (Martindale, 1989). By contrast, other dementia sufferers seem to slip into a contented dementia, somehow secure in the knowledge that they will be "held".

It may be helpful at this point to assert that there is more than one pathological process in dementia. In fact, there are several, which depend not only on the histological changes (the changes that take place at cellular and tissue level of brain functioning), but also the morphology, or gross anatomy, of the brain.

In Alzheimer's disease, the most common form of dementing illness, the degeneration of the cortex is the main visible pathology on CT scanning. Different parts of the cortex are associated with aspects of motor function, speech and language, and problem-solving, as well as personality and memory. Procedural memory appears to be more robust, so that automatic tasks (such as riding a bicycle) tend to be preserved long after people's ability to describe how they do things (Carlesimo, Fadda, Marfia, & Caltragione, 1995) has gone. Because it is a global loss of function, reality-testing appears to diminish at the same time as the other losses and often, at some point in the process, the patient loses awareness of what is happening to them. It is also entirely plausible, as Seiffer, Clare, and Harvey (2005) suggest, that *part* of this lack of awareness is "functional" and might represent a process of denial; an ego defence mechanism in operation to reduce the anguish of the threat of loss of self. Differing amounts of denial in patients with dementia can be observed during clinical practice and will be familiar to clinicians.

In Alzheimer's disease, the illness progresses from the present backwards in terms of memory loss. Early life experiences and first languages are often maintained until late on in the disease process. Individuals often seem more comfortable when recounting past events in early dementia, and there is scope for resolving early conflicts in that time. Indeed, it is arguable that they may be more available to an analytic process during this early period when they become more focused on their own early life. (Joan Hunter [1989] noted this when she reported group analytic therapy with elderly people with dementia.)

> Mrs B, who was referred to the service because of apparent depression and despondence, seemed to be confused at times; she also mentioned suicidal ideation on a regular basis and frequently threatened to take her own life. It was clear she was in the early stages of senile dementia, probably Alzheimer's, and was offered treatment. She did not respond favourably at all to antidepressant medication, but eventually began to see the team therapist regularly. Anxiety about her state was high and well-founded. As a result of her threatened suicide, she was managed very closely, but it was soon found to be anti-therapeutic to admit her formally.

> In the sessions she began to talk about her abandonment as a small child to an orphanage. The therapist maintained the contact despite occasional misses when Mrs B forgot the session. On those occasions, she telephoned to say that she was there waiting for Mrs B, in order to make it clear that she had not forgotten the session; rather, it was the other way round. The transference was quickly woven and soon Mrs B remembered her mother's visit to the orphanage, and likened her physical appearance to that of her therapist.

> The sessions were filled with the details of harsh home life and of mother's few visits. After a few months, previously unacknowledged anger at the abandonment appeared. In the countertransference, the therapist began to understand the anxiety experienced by the community psychiatric team, in that, in addition to the real threat of suicide, they were identifying "protectively" with the fear of being abandoned. This fear had started to re-emerge for Mrs B when she became aware (unconsciously) of her memory problems, and hence her wish to kill herself before ever having to experience such loss again, particularly being admitted to hospital or sent to a "home". The therapy continued for two years until her natural death.

The clinical illustration suggests that Mrs B did not seem to realize consciously that she was losing her memory. Mrs B's previously unacknowledged feelings of anger and abandonment had never been tackled psychotherapeutically as a younger adult. Perhaps her life might have been different had she had that opportunity. Faced with this subliminally known threat, her suicidal wish was strong, even though she never appeared to understand why she felt so self-destructive. As dementia progresses, these kinds of death wishes become much more rare, and frank suicidal behaviour is very unusual. (Appleby, 2006).

> Another example of the experience of progressive memory loss comes from the work of an art therapy colleague, who worked with a patient over a period of several months as her mind became more and more confused. This woman was unable to verbalize her unease. Instead, she expressed a great deal of anxiety in a generalized and unfocused way. She drew flowers in a repetitive and stereotyped manner. Of note was that her tulips grew more and more faint as her memory faded. In the therapy, she was able to make links with her picture and her anxiety about this increasingly fading self.

The other common type of pathology seen in dementia is of the vascular, or multi-infarct, variety. In vascular dementia, the blood vessels which supply the brain are occluded by the disease process at the most minute level. This results in tiny parts of the brain being starved of oxygen and nutrients, which causes their death. The "infarcts", or areas of brain death, are distributed across the cortex and the sub-cortex, including mid-brain regions and those more closely associated with emotions than the neo-cortex.

The resultant clinical picture is one of a much more patchy degeneration of memory and other skills. The loss of memory need not be retrograde, as in Alzheimer's, and indeed may disrupt early memories. The awareness of loss is more acute and present than in dementia of the Alzheimer's type, and people often become profoundly depressed for some considerable time before and during the overt part of the condition. In fact, the term "vascular depression" has been proffered as the cause of some depressions in late life that are refractory to physical treatments (Baldwin & O'Brien, 2002). These types of depression are also at greater risk of relapse (Thomas, Kalania, & O'Brien, 2004). The white matter is differentially affected in multi-infarct dementia, disrupting fibres between nerve cells, so that pathways to groups of neurones are blocked. The awareness of progressive dementia is a significant aetiological risk factor in depression, but researchers have reported a much greater risk when the sub-cortical white matter changes occur in the left cerebral hemisphere (Iosifescu et al., 2006). There is a clear tension between the role of organic disruption directly affecting emotion circuits of the limbic system and the experience of memory loss and loss of memories affecting mood.

Other writers, such as Grotjahn (1938) have mooted the possibility that dementia may disrupt the internal object relations. Evans (2004) described a series of patients who appeared to have lost "the capacity to be alone". It seems possible that this kind of relatively early (in terms of the dementia process) anxiety relating to loss of internal objects, or to an impaired ability to retain previously introjected good objects, is a consequence of a more haphazard destruction of neurones as occurs in vascular dementia, particularly that of the sub-cortical variety. Is there a possibility of a connection with this kind of dementia and the role of the orbito-prefrontal cortex, which is implicated in the development of attachment behaviour (Fonagy, Gergely, Jurist, & Target, 2004; Schore, 2003)?

The loss of the capacity to reminisce may also be an important factor in the development of depression in patients with multiple infarct dementia, as the early life experiences are just as vulnerable as the late ones, as opposed to that retrograde amnesia that tends to predominate in Alzheimer's. The patient then loses the reflective quality on past relationships, which has been proposed as an important self-object function in late old age and early dementia (O'Connor, 1994).

Conclusion

There is a great deal of evidence that an unconscious mental life continues in even very severe dementia. Early on in the dementia process, the unconscious appears to be closer to the surface, or is possibly less well defended by repressive forces. In addition, older people's egos may be more resilient, having survived this far, to the neuroses of younger adulthood. They negotiate the will to continue their existence despite ill health and loss. In the majority of dementias, people with secure attachments and a rich supply of good introjected objects and enough "mirroring self-objects" are likely to fare better. In the early stages of dementia, there may be some scope for revisiting past difficulties and losses, and even for resolving some conflicts.

Disease has no respect for good foundations, however, and it is entirely plausible that even those with a history of secure attachments might sustain an attack at the very heart of those foundations, destroying their internalized objects during the indiscriminate attacks of multiple infarct dementia.

Working with dementia sufferers using an analytic framework, which is based on an acceptance of unconscious processes, enriches the task. It improves the quality of life for all concerned, and might provide another window through which to understand the mind, in all of its many states.

References

Appleby, I. (2006). Personal communication.

Baldwin, R., & O'Brien, J. (2002). Vascular basis of late onset depressive disorder. *British Journal of Psychiatry, 180*: 157–160.

Bick, E. (1986). Further considerations on the function of the skin in early object relations. Findings from infant observations integrated into child and adult analysis. *British Journal of Psychotherapy, 2*(4): 292–299.

Carlesimo, G. A., Fadda, L., Marfia, G. A., & Caltragirone, C. (1995). Explicit memory and repetition priming in dementia: evidence for a common basic mechanism underlying conscious and unconscious retrieval deficits. *Journal of Clinical and Experimental Neuropsychology, 17*(1): 44–57.

Damasio, A. R., Damasio, H., & Van Hoesen, G. W. (1982). Prospagnosia: anatomic basis and behavioural mechanisms. *Neurology,* (32): 331–341.

Davenhill, R., Balfour, A., Rustin, M., Blanchard, M., & Tress, K. (2003). Looking into later life. Psychodynamic observation and old age. *Psychoanalytic Psychotherapy, 17*(3): 253–266.

Evans, S. (1998). Beyond the mirror: a group analytic exploration of late life depression. *Aging and Mental Health, 2*: 94–99.

Evans, S. (2004). Attachment in old age: Bowlby and others. In: S. Evans & J. Garner (Eds.), *Talking Over the Years: A Handbook of Dynamic Psychotherapy in Older Adults* (pp. 43–56). London: Routledge.

Fleminger, S. (1992). Seeing is believing: the role of "preconscious" perceptual processing in delusional misidentification. *British Journal of Psychiatry, 160*: 293–303.

Fonagy, P., Gergely, G., Jurist, E., & Target, M. (2004). *Affect Regulation, Mentalisation and the Development of the Self.* London: Karnac.

Garner, J., & Evans, S. (2001). *Institutional Abuse of Older Adults.* Report CR 84. London: Royal College of Psychiatrists.

Golander, H., & Raz, A. E. (1996). "The mask of dementia": images of demented residents in a nursing ward. *Ageing and Society, 16*: 269–285.

Grotjahn, M. (1938). Dreams. *International Journal of Psychoanalysis, 19*: 494–499.

Haggstrom, T., & Norberg, A. (1996). Maternal thinking in dementia care. *Journal of Advanced Nursing, 24*(3): 431–438.

Hunter, J. (1989). Reflection on psychotherapy with ageing people, individually and in groups. *British Journal of Psychiatry, 154*: 250–252.

Iosifescu, D., Renshaw, F. P., Kyoon Lyoo, I., Perlis, R., Papkostas, G., Niernberg, A., & Fava, M. (2006). Brain white-matter hyperintuisities and treatment outcomes in major depressive disorder. *British Journal of Psychiatry, 188*: 180–185.

Kitwood, T. (1988). The contribution of psychology to the understanding of senile dementia. In: B. Gearing, M. Johnson, & T. Heller (Eds.), *Mental Health Problems in Old Age: A Reader.* London: Wiley.

Knight, R. (1986). *Psychotherapy with Older Adults.* London: Sage.

Martindale, B. (1989). Becoming dependent again: the fears of some elderly persons and their younger therapists. *Psychoanalytical Psychotherapy, 4*: 67–75.

McKenzie-Smith, S. (1992). A psychoanalytic study of the elderly. *Free Association Journal, 3*(27): 355–390.

Menzies Lyth, I. (1959). The functioning of social systems as a defence against anxiety. Reprinted in *Containing Anxieties in Institutions. Selected Essays.* London: Free Association, 1992.

O'Connor, D. (1994). The impact of dementia: a self psychological perspective. *Journal of Gerontological Social Work, 20*: 113–128.

Ploton, L. (1995). Hypothesis of the existence of an unconscious pertinent psychic life in senile demented patients. *Psychologie Medicale, 27*(3–4): 156–159.

Rustin, M. (1989). Observing infants: reflections on methods. In: L. Miller, M. Rustin, M. Rustin & J. Shuttleworth (Eds.), *Closely Observed Infants*. London: Duckworth.

Schore, A. (2003). *Affect Dysregulation and Disorders of the Self*. New York: Norton.

Seiffer, A., Clare, L., & Harvey, R. (2005). The role of personality and coping style in relation to awareness of current functioning in early-stage dementia. *Aging and Mental Health, 9*(6): 535–541.

Thomas, A., Kalania, R., & O'Brien, J. (2004). Depression and vascular disease: what is the relationship? *Journal of Affective Disorders, 79*: 81–95.

Waddell, M. (2000). Only connect: developmental issues from early to late life. *Psychoanalytic Psychotherapy, 14*: 239–252.

CHAPTER EIGHT

Discussion of Sandra Evans' chapter: "Where is the unconscious in dementia?"

Margot Waddell

F rom the arresting opening two paragraphs of this chapter, there can be no question about where the unconscious is in dementia: it is everywhere; indeed, its workings could be said to be especially evident at this point in a person's life. By the end of the chapter we are left in very little doubt about the significance of psychoanalytic insight into these opaque states of mind. Perhaps that would have been to Freud's surprise, but more recent psychoanalytic developments into the origin and nature of deeply disturbed mental states offer considerable insight into both the states themselves and into ways of engaging with them. None the less, it has to be said that we remain in the foothills in terms of understanding this perplexing and challenging area. Both Sandra and I are in agreement that one way forward is through the application of psychoanalytic understanding.

The first example of the dementing old lady and her capacity to be alone—"she has herself to be with"—gives evidence of an internally supportive presence who relieves any sense of loneliness. The terrified, persecuted elderly man has no such benign internal figure. It looks very much as though he has dealt with anxiety, perhaps all along, by extreme splitting and projection, leaving him now at the mercy of what are felt to be hostile and attacking external enemies, in reality reflective versions of himself. There could hardly be a more poignant and graphic representation of extreme projective identification, for here, in his demented state, it is the actual self who is experienced as the malign intruder rather than the other. Here, the person into whom those threatening and unwanted parts are being projected is literally and wholly identified with the projecting self.

The process described here with such clarity is one that will be familiar to any of us who have worked or lived with dementia. As parts of the mind are lost, and with them the ability to reality-test, not only does the capacity to remember, to think, to speak, break down, but also those well-honed "defences" which have, in their respective ways, protected the personality from "too much reality" and have enabled a person to develop in his or her own unique way.

Some would call what happens "the return of the repressed", of that which, by relegation to the unconscious, enabled the personality to survive more or less intact. In dementia, or perhaps I should say in the dementias, this defensive mechanism gives way, leaving the person a prey to all manner of torments. If protected by securely established internal objects, and if, in turn, supported by sufficiently receptive and responsive external ones, some of the impact of the collapse of secondary processes, in Freudian terms, back into primary ones, can be withstood. Without this protection the person is left at the mercy of utterly chaotic, uninhibited, and persecutory internal forces.

Sandra Evans speaks with great sensitivity about the impact of these very disturbed states on the carers; often, as she points out, ill-trained and underpaid shift workers if institutionalized, or hard-pressed and distressed relatives, if at home. She mentions the carers' own life experiences with child-rearing as relevant. This I would certainly wish to confirm and to elaborate by drawing on a rather different, but in my view very helpful, psychoanalytic model: that is, Bion's theory of thinking (1962a,b) and his notion that the development of embryonic thought is lodged, initially, in the container–contained relationship between infant and mother.

The degree to which early anxieties have been projected, modulated in the mind of a reflective mother (who is, in turn, drawing on her own internalized parents), and then reintrojected by the infant in manageable form, is crucial. For, in good circumstances, the baby takes in not just the fears-made-tolerable, but also that same maternal function that has made the process possible in the first place. The individual can then draw on these same maternal capacities in nurturing relationships with his or her own children and can, perhaps, later on, better bear the angry/hostile/needy/helpless projections of the elderly, too. To a degree, such a carer may be able to understand what the projections signify and respond to them in a meaningful way. To the attentive observer, it is quite clear that this hunger for meaning extends throughout life—with particular poignancy in old age. Understanding the feelings of those with little remaining capacity to express them is an essential element in the caring role, for only so can there be any sense of what mental activity *is* going on (*such* a puzzle when relying so centrally on that special capacity for observation which can take into account both external and internal-world phenomena), the kind of binocular vision described by Bion.

A carer for those in later life can provide a setting and a mental attentiveness that renders him or her available as a thinking, containing presence. Thus, the care-giver is, or can be, a container for, and a sorter of, the projected emotional fragments which, as a consequence, can become the "contained", even though, at this stage, that function may be only very temporarily sustained. The care of the very elderly and demented, those so often lacking the capacity to speak yet so intensely riven by extreme emotional states, requires a painful reversal of the original pattern of container–contained (the younger now struggling to offer states of reverie to the old).

As Sandra Evans so rightly points out, "attempts to understand through empathy another's experience is, arguably, the most important aspect of our humanity". She also rightly draws attention to the characteristic and all too frequent "tendency towards projecting unwanted or disavowed feelings into, or on to, the most mentally vulnerable, whether in hatred, frustration, or at times disgust". This is often on the part of the carer, but it may also be on the part of the elderly themselves, those who are terrified of falling into a similar condition or who, as Evans interestingly suggests, are, at times, aware of the special status of people with dementia who are allowed "freedom not to conform".

Of particular importance in the present context is Evans' recognition of ongoing mental activity even in very advanced stages of dementia. Mysterious and perplexing experiences by many people attest to all manner of phenomena which defy tidy explanation or conceptualization. I was told by a patient recently that two days before she died, her mother, who had lived speechless, apparently mindless, and wholly dependent for well over a year, held a relatively coherent "conversation" with her. It was about whether the nurses in the care home were fond of her. This kind of anxiety, I was told, had beset my patient's mother all her life (although it was normally carefully concealed beneath the social *mores* of middle-class English society). It was New Year, and she thought she would fancy a glass of wine, the old lady said. There followed a tender enquiry into my patient's own well being, betokening a concern and interest not expressed for some years.

I cite this moving account in the context of the attention that Sandra Evans draws to Seiffer, Clare, and Harvey's work (2005), suggesting that part of the apparent lack of awareness on some people's part of what is happening to them is "functional" and may represent a process of denial, an ego defence mechanism in operation to reduce the anguish of frustration and irreversible loss, the anguish of unbearable psychic pain. It might be, when very near death, that this particular defence mechanism can be relinquished, allowing much more recognizable aspects of the personality briefly to emerge. This patient's mother died only two days after the rather lucid conversation just described, having meanwhile lapsed into a semi-comatose state.

In my own experience, it is often an unresolved oedipal situation that emerges when the protections of habit and assumptive ability and capacity fall away. A brief example will corroborate Sandra Evans' descriptions of the way in which unconscious phantasies of abandonment, insecurity, or abject dependency can re-emerge and exercise a similar kind of persecutory grip on the personality as they had in infancy and young childhood.

I shall clarify this tendency with a brief vignette, which I have written about elsewhere. (Waddell, 2002). I bring it not just for its illustrative value, but because it draws attention to a crucial tool for understanding obscure mental states: that of reflective observation. It describes how eighty-nine-year-old Mrs Brown suffered intense jealously over her belief that her husband, Eric, ninety years old and faithful for nearly sixty years of marriage, had become attracted to their recently widowed eighty-year-old friend, Gladys. When asked, one Sunday lunchtime, why she was being so uncharacteristically quiet, Mrs Brown described "the miserable time she had had the previous evening at dinner". Mrs Brown had set forth with her husband to try to cheer Gladys up. She said that the evening had been dreadful because it was clear that her hostess was "just waiting for me to die so that she can move in with Eric". As Mrs Brown reported her suspicions, she looked anxiously at her husband, who seemed puzzled, apparently not understanding what she was suggesting. He simply commented that he would not want to put up with "all Gladys's awful relatives". Mrs Brown was far from reassured. Only on close and explicit questioning did her husband add that the widow, too, was awful, and absolutely out of the question as a potential partner. His wife relaxed and began to talk animatedly and coherently about the current political situation.

A year or so later, most ordinary communication had ceased to be possible, and the central issue for Mrs Brown had become an agonizing struggle with an ever-recurring collapse of the characteristics of depressive position thinking back into a much more paranoid–schizoid state. Unlike earlier times, when Mrs B could swiftly re-emerge from a persecutory state, as we have just seen, she was now in danger of remaining cut off from those about her by the seemingly impossible road blocks of old age. Not only was she becoming cut off from others, but also from herself.

On this occasion the observer arrived to find Mr and Mrs Brown and one of their sons pottering in the kitchen. Mrs Brown was sitting holding a yellow, checked washing-up cloth. There was a bit of rubbish lying in front of her on the table. She pointed to the cloth questioningly, as if to say, "Where does this go?" and looked at Eric. Misunderstanding her "question", and thinking that she was referring to the rubbish, Eric replied, slightly impatiently, "Over there", nodding towards the bin. His wife stared at him uncomprehendingly, seeming to know that something was wrong but not being able to work out what it could be. She demurred. Fleetingly, she glanced down at the cloth and then at herself. "That's a terrible thing to say," she muttered. Ignoring this comment (Mrs Brown clearly thinking that he had meant that she herself was a piece of rubbish), Eric insisted irritably, "In there, in the proper place." She looked unhappy and continued to dither, arousing further irritation in her husband, who quite suddenly left the room. Her son put the rubbish in the bin and also left the room, without, on this occasion, the emotional resources to pause and try to understand what the problem really was.

Later, Eric found the yellow, checked cloth carefully folded and placed on top of the bin. Recalling the incident he described himself as feeling very guilty: his wife had so wanted to be obedient and to do the right thing, but had been unable to sort out her muddle between the rubbish, herself, and the cloth. She had tried to follow instructions but was mystified by her residual sense that the yellow checked cloth was *not* something that should be put in the bin, and nor, indeed, was she herself, although her life-long tendency to feel like rubbish had temporarily taken on a confused but all too concrete reality for her.

What Sandra Evans' paper so effectively lays out is something of the ways in which psychoanalytic knowledge of early development and of the nature of conscious and unconscious mental functioning have a place in, and can contribute very immediately to, the care and understanding of enfeebled or demented states of whatever kind, and to finding meaning in some of those opaque and bizarre ways of communicating that might be all that remains.

References

Bion, W. R. (1962a). A theory of thinking. *International Journal of Psychoanalysis, 43*: 306–310. Reprinted in Bion, W. R. (1967) *Second Thoughts*. London: Heinemann.

Bion, W. R. (1962b). *Learning from Experience*. London: Heinemann.

Seiffer, A., Clare, L., & Harvey, R. (2005). The role of personality and coping style in relation to awareness of current functioning in early-stage dementia. *Aging and Mental Health, 9*(6): 535–541.

Waddell, M. (2002). *Inside Lives: Psychoanalysis and the Development of the Personality*. London: Karnac.

INDEX